The Way to Wholeness

The Way to Wholeness

A Guide to Christian Self-Counseling

Frans M. J. Brandt

CROSSWAY BOOKS • WESTCHESTER, ILLINOIS
A DIVISION OF GOOD NEWS PUBLISHERS

Copyright © 1982 by Dr. Frans M. J. Brandt

First published under the title *The Renewed Mind* by Wesselhoeft Associates, Inc., Oscoda, Michigan

This new and revised edition published by Crossway Books, Westchester, Illinois.

First printing, 1984.

Printed in the United States of America

Library of Congress Catalog Card Number 84-70657

ISBN 0-89107-316-7

For my son Gerard

"And ye shall seek me, and find me, when ye shall search for me with all your heart."　　　　　(Jeremiah 29:13)

Contents

Part Four:
A Sound Mind in a Sound Body

Part Five:
The Renewed Mind

Acknowledgments

It is with great pleasure that I acknowledge my indebtedness to all who have helped me in some way or other in the preparation of this book. I am very thankful for the continuous encouragements and prayers of my friends who saw the need for this project. While many people have helped me, I am particularly indebted to Paul Battige, B.A.; Patrick V. Demay, M.A.; Edgar Ferrell; Rev. Edward Glotfelty; Nelson Good, M.A., Psy.S.; Rebecca A. Putnam, M.M.; Shari Wagener; and Adolph J. Wesselhoeft, M.A., for helpful suggestions. I am especially grateful to Gail Wacker, without whose administrative assistance and patience this book simply would not exist. For the excellent preparation of this newly revised edition I am deeply indebted to Hope Howell and Jan Dennis of Crossway Books.

Above all I am grateful to God for giving me the opportunity and privilege to serve him.

PART ONE:

THE CONSTRUCTIVE USE OF OUR MIND

For God is not the author of confusion, but of peace. . . .
(1 Corinthians 14:33)

1 Introduction

For many decades we have had a variety of programs aimed at helping us to overcome our unhappiness, mental anguish, and emotional problems. However, in spite of these programs, and the spending of millions of dollars, we are not getting happier or healthier. In fact, it seems that frustration, sadness, loneliness, and despair are increasing. Helpful scientific discoveries, improved social legislation, increased literacy rates, and many other positive events have not been able to remove our emotional burdens. Secular humanism, with a ridiculous emphasis on man to the point of self-glorification, self-worship, and total selfishness (Vitz, *Psychology as Religion,* 1977) certainly has not resolved our quest for peace or our thirst for happiness.

Contrary to claims made by some politicians and commercial, educational, and industrial interests, the world is not becoming a better place to live. Governments, universities, industry, and commerce obviously cannot provide us with lasting answers to our mental and spiritual difficulties. The secular world cannot provide us with the mental and spiritual sustenance which we need. It is an erroneous premise to believe that others can and/or should provide us with personal happiness and fulfillment.

Obviously there are many important and necessary functions being performed by many secular institutions and organizations. Few of us would deny the necessity for governments, social legislation, or free business enterprise. The common mistake, however, is that we look to others for solutions to problems that can only be provided by ourselves.

Our difficulties are for the greater part self-induced, self-maintained, self-magnified, and self-distorted. As a result of misunderstandings, we often blame ourselves and/or others. Because we misunderstand objective reality and the lawful order in all things, we tend to blame our past and/or present environment. We continue to look to others for solutions; yet there is no human being who can help us. Since we control our brain, we also control our thinking and emotions, and are therefore directly responsible for our actions. Unless we are mentally and/or intellectually impaired, under the influence of powerful mind-altering drugs, or suffering from certain physical disorders, we can help ourselves to health and happiness with God's help.

We choose how we feel, in spite of the popular misconception that others make us happy or unhappy. People and life's events may provide circumstances for us; however, we are the ones who make the final choice. The fact that we can help ourselves to happiness or unhappiness does not mean that we are sufficient to ourselves. We do need other people, and we especially need God. Even under very trying circumstances we have a personal choice in most of the things that affect our emotions.

Why do we need Christian self-counseling? Because without Christ our so-called happiness rests only on physical, material, and other transient manifestations. Just because we are happy does not mean that this happiness is self-enhancing. Worldly happiness at best is a myth, and at worst is destructive. The happiness the world talks about is quite different from the happiness we find in God. Only spiritual happiness in the Lord is complete, lasting, unchanging, and truly valuable. Strange as it may seem to the nonbeliever, true and lasting happiness can only be found by those who walk in the Holy Spirit.

Happy people are relatively free from anxiety, doubts, fears, uncertainty, and worry, or from anger, depression, envy, guilt, hatred, hostility, and jealousy. To be free of these things, however, requires more than giving direction to our thoughts and actions. While we do not necessarily need to be loved to survive physically, we do need to be loved for ultimate happiness. We need to be understood, accepted, and respected by someone who is faithful and committed to us. We need the stability of a loving and lasting relationship that can only be provided by a living and loving God.

With objective self-counseling techniques many things are possible; with God and Christian self-counseling, *everything* is possible! With God there are no hopeless or helpless cases. All of us can attain a renewed mind (Romans 12:2) by embracing Jesus as the infinite source of everything we need. In our bipolar minds, lives, and world, there is no greater choice than the choice between good and evil—between the negative, self-destructive power of Satan, and the life-giving, positive, constructive, self-enhancing power that flows from Jesus. One is the source of all things negative and destructive, and the other is the source of all things positive and constructive.

We need to lift the veil from our eyes and see the world as it really is: aflame with crime, corruption, deceit, wanton slaughter of human beings, and a meanness and filth that is so overwhelming and so unbearable to face that we often close our eyes to it and live under the illusion that all is well, or at least not "so bad." The truth is that the world is in a very bad state, and that the brutality that goes on seemingly unhindered cannot be matched in the animal world. We need to be wary of thoughts that all is well, that there is nothing to be concerned about, that mankind is making excellent progress, etc. We need to get away from the kind of thinking that says, "You are OK, and I am OK," for the truth is that very often we are not OK at all!

The struggle that is raging is within our mind or thoughts. A major battle is being fought between forces of good and evil; and if we stand idly by, we are most certainly doomed to lose! God warns us to give up our reprobate minds, to repent, and to enlighten our blinded minds by searching for spiritual truths. He warns us to renounce our defiled minds, to free ourselves from the power of Satan, to forsake our doubtful minds, and to quit trying to walk in carnal and spiritual worlds at the same time. God is calling us to be renewed in our minds, so that we may be "transformed" by accepting the mind of Jesus Christ.

This book is written to help both believers and nonbelievers to make wise choices. In Deuteronomy 30:19, 20 we read:

> I call heaven and earth to record this day against you, that I have set before you life and death, blessing and cursing: therefore choose life, that both thou and thy seed may live: that thou mayest love the Lord thy God, and that thou mayest obey his voice, and that thou mayest cleave unto him: for he is thy life, and the length of thy days.

Again, in Joshua 24:15 we are admonished to choose whom we will serve, and in Isaiah 7:15 we are urged to refuse evil and to choose good. Indeed throughout the Scriptures we are reminded to choose wisely—not to be carnally minded and choose death, but to be renewed in our minds so that we may live to the fullest extent now and always. Prophets and apostles of God, philosophers, and scientists have for centuries beseeched us to come to our senses and to help ourselves to the truth which will make us free.

Concerning the principles expressed in this book, we will be rewarded according to the amount of study and application we put forth. The concepts have been field-tested over several years and have proven to be a very effective and efficient means by which many people are helping themselves to achieve their dearest goals. God wants us happy and has done everything that is necessary for our happiness. He is merely admonishing us, pleading with us, and exhorting us not only to have faith, but to activate that faith so we may partake of the fullness of life.

If any of you lack wisdom, let him ask of God, that giveth to all men liberally, and upbraideth not; and it shall be given him. (James 1:5)

2 Christian Reeducative Self-Counseling

Christian Reeducative Self-Counseling is a practical method of emotional self-help, based on the Scriptures and proven facts about the human mind and body. God tells us throughout the Scriptures that we are responsible for our thinking, feeling, and behavior. He also teaches us how we can learn to make wise choices and lead happy and healthy lives. Philosophy, psychology, and science also show us that we are, in a sense, to take charge of our own lives, and that there is no one in heaven or on earth who will do this for us. There is no doubt whatsoever that God has placed us squarely in the driver's seat and expects us to be the driver and not the passengers in our journey through life.

Since we are forced to choose, it is obvious that we need to learn how to make the best possible choices. Christian Reeducative Self-Counseling teaches us how to make wise choices and do those things which are self-enhancing. Because we can counsel ourselves rationally and/or irrationally, it is important that we learn to distinguish between these two forms of self-counseling. Obviously we should practice the kind of self-counseling that will help us to lead the kind of lives that we want to live.

Much of Christian Reeducative Self-Counseling is based on

the work of other specialists, who have so clearly pointed out that what is needed first and foremost is a change in our thinking. As long as we believe that our unhappiness is caused by things which we cannot understand or control, there is no hope for positive self-change.

For example, Dr. Maxie C. Maultsby, Jr. (*Help Yourself to Happiness,* 1975) likes to emphasize that the world is an orderly place, and that everything always happens in accordance with strict laws. It is self-defeating to expect things to be different than they are. In other words, for anything to happen we need certain prerequisites. Many times we are doing everything that is necessary to feel miserable, yet we still believe that we should feel good. Dr. Maultsby has described in detail that behind most of our unhappiness we can find rather easily identifiable self-defeating attitudes and beliefs.

The Scriptures teach us that whatever we are is the result of our thinking (Proverbs 23:7). It is mostly what we think that leads to our feelings, be they positive, negative, neutral, or a combination of these three. It is also true, however, that our physical condition may affect our minds, and we will look closer at this later. In the meantime, we can rest assured that as long as we go through life "awfulizing," demanding, and catastrophizing, we will suffer from a number of disturbances, including anger and depression. Dr. Aaron T. Beck (*Cognitive Therapy and the Emotional Disorders,* 1979) has found that most depressive illness is based on thought disturbances, such as magnification, misinterpretation, and negative interpretation. According to Dr. Beck, depression is usually based on a deviation from logical and realistic thinking resulting in a negative self-image, ideas of deprivation, and the exaggeration of problems and difficulties.

Another well-known therapist, Dr. Paul A. Hauck (*Overcoming Depression,* 1976) stresses that there are three primary reasons for depression: self-blame, self-pity, and/or other-pity. We often see ourselves as not capable, intelligent, competent, etc. As the result of blaming ourselves for things over which we have no control in the first place, we may come to see ourselves as worthless. If we have too much self-pity, we may also have a tendency to hold others responsible for our difficulties and come to believe that these difficulties should not have happened to us. The other-pitier is well-known to all of us. When we begin to wallow in other people's problems and become too upset about their disturbances, we usually wind up being totally ineffective and just as disturbed as they are. To break a leg just because someone else has done so would not make any sense. However, emotionally we do this frequently.

Whether we look at the Scriptures, or at the work of well-known therapists, it is very clear that we can find lasting peace and happiness only when we make wise decisions. Christian Reeducative Self-Counseling helps us to greater self-understanding and teaches us the road to self-mastery. As I pointed out in *A Rational Self-Counseling Primer* (1979) most of us, most of the time, are quite capable of helping ourselves. We need only average intelligence, an open mind, and a sincere desire for positive change. In addition, we need to increase our faith and to work diligently at the conscious process of making wise decisions and choices. There is no magic in charting our own course; it is hard work!

We can find encouragement in the fact that while we may do some stupid and ignorant things, and may have several physical, intellectual, and emotional disturbances, we are nevertheless God's children and thus neither hopeless, nor worthless. We are very capable of growth and positive change. It is very important to have a positive attitude; however, it is essential to realize that Christian Reeducative Self-Counseling is based on objective thinking. It is not good to indulge in positive thinking unless there is an objective basis for it. In Christian Reeducative Self-Counseling we need to ensure that our thinking is as objective as possible. Also, we need to be sure that it is life- and health-preserving, goal-achieving, allowing us to feel the way we want to feel, and that it prevents significant conflict with our immediate environment (Maultsby, *Help Yourself to Happiness,* 1975).

It seems that most people want to survive as happily and as comfortably and as long as possible. It is this insight which provides us with a philosophy of life based on reason and respect for life in all its forms. The more reasonable our philosophy of life, the greater will be our tolerance for ourselves as

well as for others. Love is the key word in Christian Reeducative Self-Counseling, for it is only through love that we can
hope to do the will of God and understand him. Love is of God
(1 John 4:7), and God is love (1 John 4:16). It is the will of God
that we love him, love ourselves, and love others. It is love
manifested in such things as faithfulness, commitment, understanding, compassion, acceptance, and respect that will make
us free. Love will liberate us from bondage, doubts, and fear, for
God has made it quite clear that "There is no fear in love; but
perfect love casteth out fear: because fear hath torment. He that
feareth is not made perfect in love" (1 John 4:18). How self-
defeating we are as Christians, how unable to reach our goals, if
we fail to understand that love is the most important of all
things, whether on earth or in heaven. Love is the only endur-
ing quality. Love is more precious than any of God's gifts;
everything shall pass away, except love (1 Corinthians 13).

It is essential to understand that it is only through love that
we can know God (1 John 4:8) and only through practicing
love that he can dwell in us (1 John 4:12). Only through love
can we do the will of God (1 John 4:21). Jesus makes it perfectly clear that the mark of the Christian is love: "A new commandment I give unto you, That ye love one another; as I have
loved you, that ye also love one another. By this shall all men
know that ye are my disciples, if ye have love one to another"
(John 13:34, 35). Our objective is to be renewed in our minds
(Romans 12:2), so that we may move from the carnal world
into the spiritual world, so that we may indeed be "transformed" and do God's will.

In order to be fully alive, we need to be filled with love and
to share this love with others. It is only when we reach out to
others that our problems and difficulties begin to disappear.
The more we are involved with the process of Christian reeducation, the more proficient we will become in solving most of
our problems. Our lives will also reflect the kind of modeling
that is useful and beneficial to others. With an increasing will-
ingness to be reasonable in all things, and a steadfast searching
for objectivity, it becomes easier to understand, accept, and live
the wisdom of the Stoic philosopher Epictetus, who said, "It is
not things themselves that disturb men, but their ideas about
things."

According to Epictetus, the educated person does not blame others or himself. This Stoic philosopher's insights are quite scientific. It is well-known that it is not possible for two human beings to experience facts and/or events in an identical manner. Each of us has his own distinct and unique perceptual-cognitive field, or field of awareness. Our perceptions are not and cannot be identical. Why? Because our genetic makeup, our upbringing, and all of life's experiences freely intermingle with climatic, ecological, physiological, and scores of other factors that influence us to some extent. Add to this intermingling our wishes, dreams, hopes, attitudes, beliefs, etc., plus the perceptual differences based on physiological changes due to disease and the maturation process (some of our behavior is not learned!). It is simply impossible for two persons to have the same phenomenal field. In plain English, this means that it is utter stupidity and ignorance to demand that others perceive, think, feel, and act just like we do.

Jesus never had a problem in making a distinction between the person and his or her behavior, and consequently he could associate with all kinds of people and forgive them and love them. Only through forgiving can we have goodness. How self-defeating is our behavior when we believe that we are better than others. It is so obvious that all of us are fallible. While there is no doubt about our fallible nature, there is also no doubt that we need to make a distinction between a human being and his or her specific fallibilities. Obviously a "D" student is not the same as a "D" person. It is important that we learn to understand, accept, and respect one another. Yes, we need to strive for perfection, as this is clearly the will of God (Matthew 5:48). However, it seems very evident that this perfection is one of total loving and forgiving. Striving for perfection is one thing; however, to insist that we must be and can be perfect is dangerous and will lead to emotional disturbances. The simple truth is that it cannot be done.

One of the things we learn in Christian Reducative Self-Counseling is that it is self-defeating to be a perfectionist, to demand that we must be perfectly competent, qualified, and achieving in everything we do. We need to learn that we are not God and that we are not superhuman beings. After reading this book, some people will be quite amazed that they can love themselves regardless of what others think about them and regardless if they reach their goals or not.

In Christian Reeducative Self-Counseling we learn to attack self-defeating beliefs. These are the kind of beliefs that have no objective basis, but we are so used to them that we often fail to recognize them. One way by which we may learn to recognize self-defeating beliefs is by their musts, shoulds, and oughts, which frequently lead to demanding and whining and eventually to anger and self-pity. In Christian Reeducative Self-Counseling we learn that people and things do not control our happiness (or unhappiness), but that we have a choice in the matter. We learn that we do not have to remain upset with fearsome realities and that our childhood experiences do not have to determine our emotional lives of today and tomorrow.

These are not truths discovered by Stoic philosophers, as sometimes is mistakenly believed. The Scriptures have always emphasized that we have a choice, and that while things may be quite different from what we would like them to be, they are not necessarily awful, horrible, terrible, or disastrous. We read in 2 Corinthians 4:8-10, "We are troubled on every side, yet not distressed; we are perplexed, but not in despair; persecuted, but not forsaken; cast down, but not destroyed; always bearing about in the body the dying of the Lord Jesus, that the life also of Jesus might be made manifest in our mortal flesh." The more we reeducate ourselves physically, mentally, and spiritually, the less often we will blame others for our problems and difficulties. In fact, we will become increasingly honest with ourselves and more competent to solve our problems.

At the heart of Christian Reeducative Self-Counseling, we find that we are dealing with an objective analysis of our perceptions, thinking, feeling, and behavior. Such an objective self-analysis is based on the three parts of a complete emotion: (1) the *facts* and *events* (our perceptions); (2) our *self-talk* (our thoughts, attitudes, beliefs, etc., in relation to the facts and events); and (3) our *emotive feelings*. What is so beautiful and directly worthwhile in objective self-analysis is that we can quickly make sure that our *perceptions are as factual* as we can possibly determine, that our *thoughts (self-talk) are as objective* as possible, and that our *feelings are the ones we really want* to experience. The objective self-analysis makes it so very clear that it is our thinking that will determine how we feel, just as we read in Proverbs 23:7: "For as he thinketh in his heart, so is he."

Christian Reeducative Self-Counseling will help us to become more sensitive and alert to our fallibilities, as well as to our potentialities, and will help us to become less self-centered, less selfish, less mechanistic, and less fatalistic. Christian Reeducative Self-Counseling helps us to move from destructiveness to constructiveness, from negative thinking to positive thinking, from self-defeating thinking and behavior to self-enhancing thinking and behavior. Christian Reeducative Self-Counseling is in accordance with the Scriptures and follows the admonition of Paul (Romans 12:2), "And be not conformed to this world: but be ye transformed by the renewing of your mind, that ye may prove what is that good, and acceptable, and perfect will of God."

Christian Reeducative Self-Counseling is an efficient counseling method, based not only on the Scriptures but also on recent scientific evidence. It is a highly optimistic and positive way of viewing the world. It not only tells us that we are capable of change, but shows us step-by-step how to do this. Christian Reeducative Self-Counseling fits in with the glad tidings of the gospel, for it tells us that we do not have to be in bondage and that much of our stupidity, ignorance, and unhappiness can be eradicated from our lives.

It is a wonderful thing to look at the world objectively, yet with hope, faith, and love. One of Boris Pasternak's poems tells us that life is so short that it is "only an instant, only the dissolving of ourselves in the selves of all others." Before we go out into the world, freely dissolving our lives in the lives of other human beings, we may first want to take an inventory and perhaps make some changes.

Christian Reeducative Self-Counseling makes excellent sense because it is based on the Word of God, our living source of perpetual truth. Whatever we are today is primarily the result of our educational experiences. Whatever we have learned, however, we can also unlearn, relearn, or change through the reeducation process. All counseling and therapy is essentially reeducative in nature and design. Furthermore, all counseling and therapy ultimately is self-counseling. We are the only ones who directly deal with and are responsible for our minds. We are the ones who direct our brains. We may listen to others, totally or in part; we may follow their suggestions and advice; we may do a variety of other things. But when all is said and done, the final truth is that we change ourselves.

The ultimate objective is to discover that there is but one truth, and anyone who seeks diligently shall find that truth and be made free (John 8:32). God continues to call us to take charge over our lives, to make wise choices, to be responsible, to be capable, to receive power from on high. Everything has been provided. All of the tools are ready and at hand. God has already done his complete part. The waiting is on us. We have the means of understanding and altering our behavior in a self-enhancing, growth-producing manner. In so doing, we gain an increased understanding of others, helping us to appreciate and accept them without fear.

Christian Reeducative Self-Counseling rejects those humanistic theories that want us to believe that we are the end-product of history—the innocent victims of an accident in the night, cruel fate, or the final manifestation of past and present conditioning. We are far more than puppets on a string, far more than mere robots. It is true that all of us have a biological inheritance, and that many of us have organic weaknesses, diseases, and disturbances that we have simply inherited. There is no doubt that we carry around with us myriads of problems that found their early beginnings in childhood, adolescence, or even adulthood. However, we believe that those who see human beings merely as the lawful inheritors of a chain of evolutionary events, and the end-product of social development, etc., are making the cardinal error of overestimating the power of the environment, as well as underestimating the power of our mind and, worse, the power of the Holy Spirit.

Christian Reeducative Self-Counseling believes in the freedom of the mind to choose and the limitless power of the Holy Spirit. Because we accept responsibility for our thinking, feelings, and behavior, we reject the theory that we are wholly determined by our past. We believe in our educability and reeducability, and in voluntary change. We stand firm on premises of both faith and reason. Our mental lives need to be based on reason, and our spiritual lives need to be based on faith. There is neither conflict nor competition between the mind and spirit of a Christian.

Christian Reeducative Self-Counseling operates from a premise of health rather than pathology, which is unlike many other therapy and counseling modalities. In this book we shall hopefully make it clear that it is unnecessary, and sometimes dangerous, to dwell too much in the past, e.g., through so-called talk-therapies. Our emphasis is on the present and future. Our approach is one of hope, faith, and love.

It is clear that our past is important and that there are many factors in both our past and present environments that we may allow to influence us. Nevertheless, we are, to a very great extent, free to choose who we feel! Although there are no bad or good people (those with *only* bad or *only* good characteristics), there nevertheless are bad and good "behaviors." This is not the kind of badness or goodness which is based on subjective evaluations, but rather those which can stand the test of time and of all civilized cultures and societies. For example, good behavior is the kind of behavior that is constructive. It shows practical love—that is, understanding, acceptance, and respect. It is the kind of behavior that inflicts no harm of any kind on anyone, that does not trespass, but rather helps to enhance the happy survival of others. Bad behavior is the other kind of behavior. It is not love, but rather hatred and hostility that is practiced. It does inflict harm on others, it does trespass, and it hinders or prevents the happy survival of others. Having these behaviors does not make us good or bad, for as long as we are in our mortal bodies we remain fallible. Clearly there is not one of us who can point a finger at anyone else. The Scriptures tell us that "all have sinned, and come short of the glory of God" (Romans 3:23).

While we can love and accept human beings, it is incorrect to assume that we need to agree passively with destructive behaviors, or go out of our way to justify certain destructive behaviors as the result of things that are allegedly beyond our control. Nothing could be further from the truth. In fact, irresponsibility and fear of reality—or worse, denial of reality—is already responsible for a great deal of misery and unhappiness (Glasser, *Reality Therapy,* 1975).

Christian Reeducative Self-Counseling is not suited for those who are mentally and/or intellectually seriously impaired, or those who take heavy doses of mind-altering drugs, including alcohol. Those people, until they are in remission, are unlikely to have the necessary control over their minds to choose appropriately, make wise decisions, and give direction to their lives. We must be careful, however, to realize that most people, most of the time, are capable, and that far too many people are incarcerated in institutions against their will who could function very well on their own and who would be more capable of making sound decisions if taken off their deadly drugs.

Christian Reeducative Self-Counseling is really a holistic approach, for we are concerned with the entire individual. There is no doubt whatsoever that we must give careful thought to our physical as well as mental and spiritual health. Remember, there is no conflict between reason and faith. They go hand in glove together. Objective thinking will lead to sane, sound, and self-enhancing behaviors. We hope that all of us will come face to face with the reality of our situations, be they in the physical, mental, or spiritual realm.

In summary, Christian Reeducative Self-Counseling is a practical method of emotional self-help, aimed at self-realization and Christian self-enhancement. Whatever we feel and do is primarily the outcome of our thinking; however, we only translate those perceptions, thoughts, and images into behavior that corresponds to our value system. When our thinking is disturbed by self-defeating beliefs, or other thought disturbances such as magnification and misinterpretation, then emotional problems and difficulties may be the end result. Spiritual and physical problems may also lead to emotional disturbances and vice versa, necessitating a holistic point of view. The Christian Reeducative Self-Counseling approach to problem-solving and behavioral change is found in objective self-confrontation, acceptance of responsibility, and objective reality. Objectification and visualization, based on a Christian value system, will lead to inner healing, culminating in oneness with the Lord, through the renewing of our mind!

PART TWO:

THE POWER
OF OUR
MIND

Through wisdom is a house builded; and by understanding it is established. (Proverbs 24:3)

3 Faith and Reason

If there is one need that all of us have, it is the need to reason (Isaiah 1:18), and to increase our understanding and wisdom (Ecclesiastes 7:25). If we regularly and earnestly search our minds, we will find the best possible ways by which we can take care of our bodies and minds and thus better serve God, our fellowmen, and indeed ourselves (Romans 12:1, 2).

Increased understanding will lead to a more effective and efficient use of the wonderful minds that God has given us, and will greatly reduce many serious misunderstandings which often prevent us from leading more joyful lives. A typical misunderstanding is the belief that it is not necessary to use our minds when it comes to matters of faith, or that God can and will answer us even when we do everything necessary to sabotage our prayers, by not saying what we mean and not meaning what we say.

In Hebrews 11:1 we read that ". . . faith is the substance of things hoped for. . . ," and this clearly tells us that faith is not something that comes without effort. Faith requires initiation, action, and commitment on our part, and all of this takes place in our minds. Also, we do not just hope for *anything,* but rather we hope for specific things, which we have thought about, visualized in our minds, and then requested from God.

It goes beyond question that faith is the cornerstone of our religious beliefs and that it permeates all of our lives. By faith we are justified (Romans 3:28), purified (Acts 15:9), sanctified (Acts 26:18), and saved (Mark 16:16). It is through faith that we have access to God's precious gifts and promises. Faith is not something that is forced upon us, but rather it is part of the same conscious act by which we chose to become Christians.

This responsibility to choose, or the freedom to make up our own minds (Joshua 24:15), is a very serious task. Certainly there is every reason for us to choose as rationally as possible. We are forced to make many choices every day, and we know how difficult the process can be. The complexity of our world, the subjective nature of many issues we deal with, and our own fallibility make it essential that we indeed "seek out wisdom, and the reason of things, and to know the wickedness of folly, even of foolishness and madness" (Ecclesiastes 7:25).

God gave us minds so that we can choose wisely. We do not have to be driven by some blind, purposeless, or even corrupt force. Although God gives us a choice, he wants us to be guided by purposeful reasons, thoughts, feelings, and actions. We learn this from the Word of God, and we see it manifested in all of his creation.

We need faith to have access to God's promises, and as long as we prepare ourselves, we can receive these promises. In fact, the only thing that separates us from receiving any or all of his promises would be a lack of faith. Lack of faith does not come from God, but from the enemy of God, and manifests itself in negative thinking, feelings, and actions which prevent us from having faith.

Many misunderstandings in our lives are the result of self-defeating thinking, which prevents us from being happy and healthy and from reaching our goals. There is plenty of guidance by which we can help ourselves. First of all, there is God, the loving source of all things that are good for us. In fact, not only is God the source, but he tells us exactly what we need to do to be happy, successful, healthy, and everything else that is good for us, as long as we are ready and willing to ask, seek, and knock (Matthew 7:7, 8). Although God wants us to keep his commandments, he does not force us to do anything at all. God calls us, warns us, teaches us, and advises us, but it is up to us to listen or not. He wants us to choose and to take responsibility for our choices.

Secondly, there are many pastors, preachers, priests, teachers, counselors, therapists, and others who are interested in our welfare, and who may advise, counsel, guide, teach, and/or pray with us. Of course, we may spend years in so-called therapy and make no progress whatsoever. We can have the most rational advice and do the most irrational things. We can listen to the finest sermons or even be face to face with miracles and be totally unmoved. Unless we take charge of our minds, and unless we counsel ourselves, nothing can happen. Unfortunately many of us do not even believe that we have personal minds, and that we are capable of thinking and choosing wisely. This is often the unfortunate result of years of erroneous education and of listening to the voice of the enemy, who exaggerates our weaknesses and minimizes our strengths. When we are taught that we are dumb and not capable of making good decisions, then how can we be anything else but self-defeating in our thinking, feelings, and actions?

It is no wonder that many of us allow our environments (wives, husbands, children, friends, bosses, employees, etc.) to decide for us if we are going to be happy or not. When we go to work and our boss is in a bad mood, there is a good chance that we will also be in a bad mood; and when our boss is in a good mood, there is a good chance that we will also be in a good mood. This does not mean that the environment is all-powerful. It means that if we do not take charge of our minds, then we will be the self-made victims of our environment. We will feel good when people like us (deserved or not), and we will feel bad when they don't like us (deserved or not), and thus be completely at their mercy. There is no need for us to be at anyone's mercy unless we choose to do so.

While we have plenty of good sources to help us find success, there are also many sources which will help us fail. We can choose to whom we will listen, and what we will do as a result. It is only through the use of reason that we can make the decisions that are in our best interest. We can only counsel ourselves, however; we must be aware that we can do so rationally or irrationally.

It is unfortunate that we often take our minds for granted

and quite erroneously believe that our minds will take care of themselves. However, this is simply not true. Our minds need executive control, the kind of control (again by choice) that comes from living in the Holy Spirit. When left to their own devices, our minds willingly absorb all manner of nonsensical and even self-destructive information. Our minds are analogous to computers which are only as good as the programmers and operators. We need to start with the right kind of input. Garbage-in will certainly produce garbage-out!

The Apostle Paul warns us, "Be not conformed to this world: but be ye transformed by the renewing of your mind, that ye may prove what is that good, and acceptable, and perfect will of God" (Romans 12:2). We can ask God to renew our minds, but I am afraid that is not what God is telling us. He says, "Be ye transformed by the renewing of your mind." God has already done his part. We don't have to convince him of our need to renew our minds; he is waiting for us to do our part. He wants us to do self-counseling, to choose, decide, reason, and learn to be responsible. It is up to us to do our part, and he will not refuse us anything he has promised. It is up to us to lead lives that are pleasing to God and beneficial to others and ourselves.

To succeed with Christian Reeducative Self-Counseling, we need faith so that we can have the "substance of things hoped for." But of course we need to be involved and committed. Now, what are those things in the world that we don't want to be conformed to? What is there in our lives that we want to change? Do we know that *our* thinking is responsible for *our* feelings and actions? Thus, our minds directly control such things as language, drinking, drug-taking, smoking, overeating, anger, fear, jealousy, etc., and of course also of all the positive things that we feel and do. We are simply the end-product of our thoughts (Proverbs 23:7). Clearly, it is crucial that we learn to think about our thinking. We need to start paying full attention to the importance of our thoughts, and more specifically to the words that make up those thoughts.

Do we really wish to renew our minds and do the "good, acceptable, and perfect will of God"? If so, then we need to pay special attention to those things that will prevent us from reaching that goal. Negative and destructive thoughts, and anything else that severs or hinders our relationship with God, need to be looked at. In fact, any thought, feeling, or action which harms our bodies or minds so that we are no longer "a living sacrifice, holy, acceptable to God" (Romans 12:1) is certainly against the will of God.

It is the will of God that we keep his commandments and have full access to all of his gifts and promises. We become Christians and obtain everlasting life through our belief in Jesus (John 3:16; 3:36), but we live Christian lives through commitment and active participation in the will of God. It is the will of God that we love him, and we need to be mindful that he loved us first. In Isaiah 53:5 we read that ". . . he was wounded for our transgressions, he was bruised for our iniquities: the chastisement of our peace was upon him; and with his stripes we are healed." God wants us to know and understand that he has done his part.

How can we do our part? As Christians we can freely partake of all his gifts and promises. However, just as we have to participate in our salvation by receiving it through faith, we need to participate in the full development of our minds and of our faith. God has provided the master plan and all of the tools we need to understand his plan and put it into practice. It is only through the use of our minds that we choose positive or negative things, constructive or destructive thoughts, success or failure, or any combination of them. If we wish to increase our faith, then we need to increase our efforts so that we may have the kind of minds about which the Apostle Paul told us. Reasoning, reasonableness, moderation, wisdom, and understanding are some of the building-stones of our minds, which will help give strength and direction to our faith.

While it is through faith that we believe, repent, are baptized, receive the Holy Spirit, and are healed, it is clear that any of this would be most difficult, if not impossible, if we are confused, fearful, intimidated by others, living in anger or hostility. It would seem that we need to be as objective as possible. It is best to look to Jesus, for he was the most rational person who ever lived on earth. He did nothing that was self-defeating. Everything Jesus did was true and objective. He did nothing harmful to his body, mind, or spirit. Even when he gave his life for us, this was a rational act, for it fulfilled the will of God and among other things led to his resurrection and glory (Luke 24:26). Jesus' life was goal-achieving and allowed him to feel the way he wanted to feel. The difficulties that he experienced with those who opposed him were not significant to him, for he endured them without destructive anger, guilt, or worry and remained steadfast. Only the Son of God can be completely rational; however, we can follow his example and strive to have as much control over our lives as is possible for us.

It is, of course, very important to have this control, for it is the only way by which we can be guided by that which is good for us, and to abstain from that which is bad for us. One of the most rational things we can do is to love God and others. He tells us, "Owe no man any thing, but to love one another: for he that loveth another hath fulfilled the law" (Romans 13:8). God loved us first—"For God so loved the world, that he gave his only begotten Son, that whosoever believeth in him should not perish, but have everlasting life" (John 3:16).

Reflecting on God's love and on his precious gifts and promises, it is certainly not much to ask that we "lead a quiet and peaceable life in all godliness and honesty" (1 Timothy 2:2). Unfortunately we often fail, and this is not necessarily because we are dishonest, but because we failed to do our homework. We failed to be renewed in our minds. When we act self-defeatingly, it is not always the result of some emotional disturbance. Often we are simply uninformed; that is, we don't know any better because we have not learned enough, or we may lack the intelligence to be more objective.

Ignorance is not really bliss! Not knowing often gets us into serious trouble with ourselves and with others. For some of our ignorance we may even have an excuse, especially as it relates to not having had an opportunity to learn. For much of our ignorance, however, we have no reasonable excuse. If we were to spend as little as thirty minutes a day, we could learn to make major improvements in our thinking, feelings, and actions. Certainly there are many misunderstandings, biases, prejudices, irrational ideas, and negative attitudes that we would do well to eliminate from our lives. It is a great misunderstanding on our part when we expect God to answer our prayers while we do everything that is necessary to sabotage these prayers by not meaning what we say and not saying what we mean.

Does it make any sense to ask God to forgive us our transgressions if we fail to accept his forgiveness? Should we ask God to help us to feel better about ourselves if we continue to blame ourselves, while all our thinking is directed toward our frequently self-induced and self-maintained sense of worthlessness? Is it reasonable to ask God to let us come home, and then go about ignoring his door which is wide open and his arms which are outstretched, because, after all, we know better than God, and declare ourselves unworthy? Can God take away our depression when we work by day and by night, making sure that we talk and talk and talk and talk some more about all the terrible, horrible, and awful things that always happen to us? When we continue to cry and whine about the past, it is unlikely that we will be renewed in our minds in the present!

In Mark 11:23 we read that we can have "whatsoever" we say, and this means all the good and beautiful things we want. However, it is also a scientific fact that when we keep talking about bad, hopeless, and negative things, we will feel and act that way. In Matthew 12:37 we read, "For by thy words thou shalt be justified, and by thy words thou shalt be condemned." God cannot answer our prayers when we do everything that is necessary for us not to be heard. It's no use asking for the things we don't want, don't need, don't believe that we will receive, or anything that goes contrary to the will of God.

For the resolution of our problems we need faith, but even our faith has to make sense. Faith does not exist in a vacuum; it is the "substance of things hoped for, the evidence of things not seen" (Hebrews 11:1). What are some of the things we hope for? What are some of the things we would like to see in our lives?

God wants us to lead joyful lives, but one of the major obstacles is our lack of faith, which may well be the result of our failure to take control over our lives. We must remember that if we don't choose, then others will do the choosing for us. Perhaps we will be pulled first left, then right, and be tossed to and fro. Our lives will lack direction, goals, and meaning. Our negative emotions may gain the upper hand and bring us much unhappiness and despair, and even prevent us from doing the will of God.

We need to know why we do what we do, why we feel the way we feel. In what ways can we have more control over our feelings and actions? Although we need more self-understanding and self-control, we are not interested in the kind of knowledge of the mind which all too often has become a kind of religion in its own right, leading to self-worship (Vitz, *Psychology as Religion,* 1977). We are not looking for self-deification or other narcissistic goals, but rather personal enhancement as children of God. We wish to be renewed in our minds, so that we can do God's will, fully partake of his promises, and improve our relationships with others. One other very important goal is to become more accepting and forgiving of ourselves and to lead more Christian lives.

Christian Reeducative Self-Counseling is an effective and efficient method which helps us to help ourselves. It is a blessing to those of us who are in need of self-understanding and self-direction. Indeed, a thorough study and application of the principles of Christian Reeducative Self-Counseling will help us to become more and more the way God would like us to be.

Purification of character, more reasonable behavior, stronger moral convictions, continued growth in the spiritual, emotional, social, and intellectual spheres—all of this can come about through the rightful combination of faith and reason. As our self-understanding increases, so will our understanding of others. As we more readily understand and accept our fallibility, so shall we be more able to accept the fallibility of others. We shall be too busy with the removal of the beam in our own eye to worry about the splinter in the eye of our brother. Accepting our fallibility does not mean that we accept our negative behavior or deny responsibility for any part of our behavior (Glasser, *Reality Therapy,* 1975). We merely gratefully acknowledge God's full acceptance of us as repenting sinners (Mark 2:17). Since God has accepted us, we need to do our part, and that is to accept ourselves. God loves us and wants us to love him, ourselves, and others. Can we really do this with whining, crying, complaining, bitterness, jealousy, or spite?

The deeper our faith is anchored in a rational mind, the more fruitful it will prove to be. Norman Vincent Peale recently made clear in *The Positive Power of Jesus Christ* (1980) that faith and positive thinking are really synonomous! Our reasoning minds will strengthen our faith by changing negative attitudes into positive ones, self-defeating attitudes into self-enhancing ones, and self-defeating beliefs into the kind of beliefs we want and that are good for us.

Let there be no mistake about it—faith is the most important of all the ingredients, for we are saved "by grace . . . through faith" (Ephesians 2:8). There is no question that faith can overcome many of the limitations of reason. Through the positive and rational use of our minds, we can quickly discover that faith only acts when we get into action, and that thinking helps us to focus better on the important guidance that we can obtain from the Word of God. Our minds are the vessels that carry the "substance of things hoped for," called faith!

. . . until ye be endued with power from on high. (Luke 24:49)

4   Mind and Holy Spirit

In the previous chapters we have talked about the importance of making good choices, and the interrelationship of faith and reason. We have also stressed that *our thinking* is primarily responsible for *our feelings* and for *our actions.* It seems so self-evident, if we only stop and think for a moment, that mind-power is synonomous with thought-power, and ultimately with word-power.

Since our thinking is primarily responsible for our feelings and actions, it is obvious that we need to pay special attention to our thinking. Our ability to think clearly is, of course, contingent on our genetic endowment, past experiences, and overall physical health. In addition to hereditary, environmental, and physical factors, our thinking is very much influenced by psychological factors—that is, by the way in which we perceive, interpret, appraise, and evaluate facts and events, whether they are in the past, present, or future.

It is an interesting fact that in spite of all the components that make up our behavior, virtually all of it is learned! Very little of our behavior is not learned. This is both exciting and good news. It tells us that if most of our behavior is learned, we can also unlearn, relearn, and change it as needed. Christian Reeducative Self-Counseling is possible only because we can learn to change our behavior, be it physical, mental, or spiritual. Thank God!

If we want to think wisely, then we need to take full responsibility for all of our thoughts, feelings, and actions. Yet, it is not enough to be responsible and to desire health and happiness. Our minds need guidance. Since thinking controls our minds we can ask, who and what is going to control our thinking? It seems strange to us that our minds do not automatically make the right choices and that we actually have to supervise our minds. Yet that's the way it is. Our minds need to be supervised by our minds. At first that may seem to be double-talk, but nothing could be further from the truth. We need to feed our minds with healthy nutrients as well as healthy thoughts.

Everything we do ultimately is the result of our thoughts. It becomes a very important matter to decide what thoughts we will feed into our minds. Most of us are more concerned about what we feed our car engines than what we feed our bodies and minds. We are usually unaware that there is such a thing as selective feeding of the mind.

We can easily prove that most of us are unaware that we are responsible for our minds. For example, if we seriously blame the environment for all of our behavior, then we are unaware of personal choice, responsibility, and opportunity. We are not end-products of our experiences or our environments. We are not merely robots or puppets. We are made by history only to the extent that we allow this to be so, particularly in the area of our spiritual and emotional happiness. For example, a serious accident may leave us physically crippled, but this does not mean that we have to also be mentally and/or spiritually crippled.

Our concern ideally is in the present rather than in the past. It is today that really counts; today we need to make wise choices. In Joshua 24:15 we read: "And if it seems evil unto you to serve the Lord, choose you *this day* whom ye will serve . . ." We have the choice, but we are reminded to make choices *today,* for obviously yesterday is gone and tomorrow does not yet exist. Even if tomorrow comes, it will not exist in the same way that today or this very moment exists. We cannot exactly duplicate history.

If our minds were the self-regulating machines that so many people erroneously believe them to be, our lives would be happy and healthy most of the time. However, it is clear that this is not so. Without guidance, our minds become doubtful, fearful, confused. What we need to do is take executive control over our minds. As Christians, we need to be directed by that "power from on high," for only in this way shall we be able to walk in the Spirit and succeed in all things good and beautiful. Yes, we need to carefully, consciously, selectively, and wisely control our minds with the guidance of the Holy Spirit.

In the Scriptures there are more than four hundred helpful references to the Holy Spirit. For example, in Ezekiel 36:27 we read: "And I will put my Spirit within you, and cause you to walk in my statutes, and ye shall keep my judgments, and do them." Certainly with the help of hundreds of Scripture references it will not be too difficult to increase our faith to the point of believing and receiving. In Romans 10:17 we read, "So then faith cometh by hearing, and hearing by the Word of God." We clearly need to activate our minds, to be participators, to be committed and receptive, to be faithful and loyal. It is only through the making of correct choices that we can learn to live Christian lives. Without healthy, optimally functioning minds that are as objective as possible, we cannot hope to walk in the Spirit. It is a well-known fact that most of the destructive and self-defeating things we do are the result of stupidity, ignorance, and emotional disturbances. The latter is directly related to the former. Emotional disturbances are very often the direct result of stupidity and ignorance.

The believer's body is the temple of the Holy Spirit (1 Corinthians 6:19) and must be properly treated (Romans 12:1), and a healthy mind is essential to walk with the Lord (Romans 12:2). The person with a doubtful mind (Luke 12:29), carnal mind (Romans 8:7), or blinded mind (2 Corinthians 3:14), or any other mind except one which is in Christ, cannot be renewed in the mind (Romans 12:2) and live a "transformed" life.

Jesus was the most rational person who ever lived on earth, and it is important to recognize that fact. The Lord was an active, thinking participant. He prayed, taught, traveled, worked, studied, resisted temptations, performed miracles, and gave executive control of his mind to the Holy Spirit. God, the Holy Spirit, and Jesus are one; yet Jesus did not merely rely on his own judgment. He constantly and consistently looked for guidance from God and walked in the Holy Spirit (Luke 4:1). It is only through the power of the Holy Spirit that we can have the kind of executive control desired by Christians. Of course, we can also give executive control of our minds to Satan; we can participate in the occult, rely on horoscopes or fortune-tellers, participate in seances, etc., or we can forget about feeding our minds entirely and continue to flounder around and be tossed from left to right, ignoring God's warning to pay attention to where we are going, so that our "ways be established" (Proverbs 4:26).

If Jesus, the son of the living God, who himself *is* God, consciously seeks guidance from God, then how much more are we in need of this! It is at our peril if we ignore our greatest need, the need to be fed spiritually. In psychology we speak a lot about the so-called hierarchy of needs, of the necessity to take care of bodily needs, safety needs, needs of belonging, and growing to our fullest potential. Yet, most modern psychologists give no thought at all to the matter of executive control over the mind. That is why they—just like their clients—so very often confuse cause and effect. For example, many if not most social scientists firmly believe that adverse economic conditions are *the* cause of increased violence, crime, perversions, and things of that nature. Yet, nothing is further from the truth. We are responsible for our behavior, and we need to give executive control over our minds to God (the ultimate force for good).

The world is an orderly place, and everything has a prerequisite. It is true that economic as well as other kinds of hardships will be a challenge—an extra burden, perhaps even a crushing one. However, we have conclusive knowledge and evidence that poverty does not breed crime. What breeds crime is the carnal mind engaging in greed, corruption, and selfishness. There is plenty of crime and corruption committed by the very rich and affluent. Crime and all its ramifications are the result of evil, of failure to give executive control over our minds to the forces of good.

Our minds are astonishingly powerful. We can resolve and overcome some of the most devastating problems through the power of our mind. People obtain healing, earn fortunes, travel in space, and overcome seemingly impossible tasks through the power of the mind. Yet, all of these feats are nothing compared to the power that comes from the Holy Spirit. In this book we will discuss some simple techniques that will enable us to overcome unhappiness, depression, anger, hatred, and many more things. Such victory is wonderful and positive. More important, we hope to learn that while we have many wonderful powers within our minds, there is a power far greater and which can yet be obtained easily and at no cost, by coming to Jesus. The Scriptures tell us that "Jesus stood and cried, saying, If any man thirst, let him come unto me, and drink. He that believeth on me, as the Scripture hath said, out of his belly shall flow rivers of living water" (John 7:37, 38).

Of course there will be rivers of living water, for it is a fact that through the Holy Spirit we literally have God within us. In the Scriptures we read, ". . . greater is he that is in you, than he that is in the world" (1 John 4:4). That is easy to understand, for the Holy Spirit who wants to live in us is God. The Holy Spirit is eternal (Hebrews 9:14), omnipotent (Luke 1:35), omniscient (1 Corinthians 2:10, 11), and omnipresent (Psalm 139:1-4). The Holy Spirit comes to us through Jesus, as explained by John the Baptist: ". . . I indeed baptize you with water; but one mightier than I cometh, the latchet of whose shoes I am not worthy to unloose: he shall baptize you with the Holy Ghost and with fire" (Luke 3:16).

Can anyone of us receive this power, this guidance, this executive control over our minds? The answer is yes! God wants all of us who believe and acknowledge Jesus as Savior to receive the Holy Spirit, at the time of salvation (Acts 10:44-48) or in some sense thereafter (Acts 19:1-7). No believer will be denied the Holy Spirit, as we read in Luke 11:13—"If ye then, being evil, know how to give good gifts unto your children; how much more shall your heavenly father give the Holy Spirit to them that ask him?" We should avoid all arguments about the Holy Spirit (Gilquist, *Let's Quit Fighting about the Holy Spirit*, 1974), and the one thing we must never do is denounce the Holy Spirit, as this is the one unforgivable sin. Jesus tells us that ". . . whosoever shall speak a word against the Son of man, it shall be forgiven him: but unto him that blasphemeth against the Holy Ghost it shall not be forgiven" (Luke 12:10).

Although many books have been written about the Holy Spirit, all we need is to accept and walk in the Holy Spirit, the Spirit of God. He will guide us and lead us, and he will help us to solve any and all problems, challenges, and difficulties. What cannot be achieved by the power of the mind can quickly be done by the power of the Holy Spirit. Many times I have witnessed some of the greatest problems of the longest standing being resolved in a few minutes by those who were willing to give total control to Jesus Christ, the Son of the living God. In that way, I have seen instant and lasting transformations, as unhappiness melted faster than snow in the searing sun.

Power of any kind comes to those who have faith. Those of us who hope, who trust, who believe, who visualize success and victory will receive power. Yet, the power of God will only come into our minds if we walk in the Holy Spirit. There is enmity between the carnal mind and the spiritual mind (Romans 8:7); and the only battle of real consequence is the battle between good and evil, between right and wrong, between Jesus and Satan, between constructiveness and destructiveness, between self-enhancing and self-defeating behavior, between happiness and unhappiness.

Now what are some of those things that cause us so much pain and unhappiness, so much turmoil, so much destruction? The Scriptures tell us they are "adultery, fornication, uncleanness, lasciviousness, idolatry, witchcraft, hatred, variance, emulations, wrath, strife, seditions, heresies, envyings, murders, drunkenness, revelings . . ." (Galatians 5:19-21). When we are in the power of any of these manifestations, we may find that we are in deep trouble. Many people are destroying their lives because of envy. Anger (wrath) is the most commonly found destructive habit in our society. Drunkenness (alcoholism) is now one of the four most serious health problems in the United States. What we need to recognize is that we cannot have God's power if we are under the control of destructive physical and/or mental habits. The drugged mind is not free. The mind placed under the influence of horoscopes, etc. is not free.

Human beings are inherently irrational. All evidence

throughout history, throughout the modern world, in our own lives, and wherever we look will testify to that fact. Left alone as infants, we will literally destroy ourselves. Left uneducated, we will not survive. It is not merely our irrational nature, however, that is the biggest problem, but rather our sinful nature, our desire to walk on the road to destruction which is paved with selfishness and greed.

Our mind is irrational and powerless when it is not properly directed. Certainly no one argues with the technical mind control of the people who supervise and fly the space shuttles. Virtually everything goes according to plan, but only because everything is supervised, guided, and controlled to the nth degree. No space shuttle goes up or comes down without a meticulous flight plan. None of us can have *The Positive Power of Jesus Christ* (Peale, 1980) and enjoy the fruit of the Spirit (Galatians 5:22, 23) unless we use God's flight plan to guide us safely.

Without knowledge we cannot fly a plane or space shuttle, and without knowledge we cannot do a good job with our lives. In Proverbs 4:5 we are told to "get wisdom, get understanding." Understanding is directly reflected in love. It is God's wish and commandment that we love him, that we love our neighbors, and that we love ourselves. God is love, and we can know God and do his will and work *only* through love. In Matthew 22:36-40 we read:

> Master, which is the great commandment in the law? Jesus said unto him, Thou shalt love the Lord thy God with all thy heart, and with all thy soul, and with all thy mind. This is the first and great commandment. And the second is like unto it, Thou shalt love thy neighbor as thyself. On these two commandments hang all the law and the prophets.

God loves us, because he understands, accepts, and respects us, and is committed to us. He loves us unconditionally. He asks that we do the same thing, so that all mankind may be one. One of the reasons we are in trouble is because we have failed to love. We have failed to love God, failed to love others, and failed to love ourselves. When we go through life blaming, pitying, whining, and crying, then we have failed to have "fervent love." In 1 Peter 4:8 we read ". . . have fervent charity [love] among yourselves: for charity [love] shall cover the multitude of sins." It is very important to learn to accept, respect, and understand ourselves *and* others as fallible human beings, and to be committed and faithful to ourselves *and* others by doing all the things that are necessary for our full development as God's children.

If we do not understand ourselves, and/or reject and despise ourselves, then we have failed to love ourselves and cannot possibly love others. How can we be happy with something we don't like, don't want, and in which we don't believe? How can we possibly be successful if we continue to believe that we are incompetent, incapable, and inadequate?

If we do not understand ourselves, then we cannot help ourselves or others, and we may continue to rely on mind-altering drugs or the excessive use of nicotine, alcohol, etc. Our sense of personal worth, our self-esteem, is directly related to our ability to love ourselves and others. This sense of personal worth, manifested in such things as love, achievement, and independence, is not merely a matter of liking ourselves because others like us. A sense of personal worth also needs freedom from the bondage and stifling habits that corrupt our bodies and minds. Our self-esteem is tied up with victory over self-defeating and self-destructing thoughts, feelings, and actions. It comes to us when we feed our minds with the proper kind of mental and spiritual food. We can soar at heights without limit when the control of our minds is directed by the Holy Spirit.

The ultimate purpose of Christian Reeducative Self-Counseling is ultimate happiness. There is no doubt that if we walk with the Lord we shall be the happiest people on earth. Happiness comes when we look above and beyond ourselves.

We are troubled on every side, yet not distressed. (2 Corinthians 4:8)

5 Troubled but Not Distressed

It may seem strange, but it is a fact: we can help ourselves immensely by helping others! The Lord promises *us* healing if we ". . . pray for one another . . ." (James 5:16). When we are busy helping others, we get involved with something that goes beyond the limitations of our own existence. Our problems become smaller and less significant. When we are concentrating on helping others, we cannot at the same time engage in negative self-talk about our own situation. We need to learn to look above and beyond ourselves. As has already been pointed out in previous chapters, we are not merely made by history: we also make history. The kind of history that we make is often very self-defeating because we spend a great deal of time literally talking ourselves into failure, depression, and all kinds of unhappiness. We erroneously believe that we are the helpless victims of some horrible childhood or adolescence or the end-products of some terrible unfairness. By seeing ourselves as puppets, it becomes easy to suffer from self-pity, self-blame, and other negative thoughts.

All too often we limit our thinking to "small" things and come to believe that our immediate environment is representative of the whole world. Also, our human ability to generalize makes it easy for us to be blinded by falsehoods. For one thing, most of us believe that what we see, hear, smell, feel, and taste is objective reality. All too often we operate more on feelings than on reason. If something feels good, we assume it to be good. If something feels bad, we assume it to be bad. We also rely excessively on our eyes and ears to tell us what is going on in the world around us. The trouble is that we overlook the fact that we do not hear with our ears, and that we do not see with our eyes, but rather we see and hear with our mind. Our sense organs merely relay perceptions to our minds, where they are received as messages, then interpreted, evaluated, sorted out, processed, and handled in a variety of other ways. It is important to realize that our sense organs are rather imperfect. Even if they are perfect (e.g., we might have so-called perfect vision), this will still not ensure accurate reception or understanding. All of the inputs we receive through our sense organs need to be evaluated by our very subjective minds. Our minds are filled with memories, rational and irrational beliefs, ideas, attitudes, prejudices, biases, fantasies, etc.

Unfortunately, what we assume to be objective reality is really something that is based on the inputs from our imperfect sense organs—i.e., inputs which have been relayed to and processed by our mind. Our mind is a storehouse of information, both accurate and inaccurate, rational and irrational. Fortunately, the more attention we give to the functioning of our mind and the harder we work at objective thinking, the greater are our chances for dealing with the truth.

When we say that we are fallible human beings, we are doing more than making a philosophical statement or making an excuse for undesirable behavior. What we are doing is acknowledging a scientific fact. All of us are very prone to misinterpret, misjudge, and misunderstand. Most of the suffering in the world is the result of misunderstandings. A great deal of our misery could be eliminated if only we better understood the working of our minds. For example, it is a very common, yet very serious misunderstanding that we have little or no control over our feelings.

Many of us believe that very little in our lives is really under our control, and that there is little if anything we can do for ourselves. There are millions of us who honestly believe that our lives are controlled by the stars, or that past events (even our dates of birth) are more powerful determinants of success and happiness than the actions we take on our own behalf.

However, this is not what we find from the study of science, philosophy, psychology, or the Scriptures. It is true that we have no control over many things in our past or present environment. It is also true that very serious difficulties and challenges may come into our lives. Yet, glory to God, we can have a tremendous choice over our feelings and learn to look above and beyond ourselves. In 2 Corinthians 4:8, 9 we read:

> We are troubled on every side, yet not distressed; we are perplexed, but not in despair; persecuted, but not forsaken; cast down, but not destroyed.

How fortunate that we have overwhelming evidence that most of us, most of the time, are quite capable of taking charge of our own lives. In fact, we are commanded to do so (Deuteronomy 30:19). God holds every one of us who is capable fully responsible for all the actions that we take (Joshua 24:15). We have been given the challenge and the opportunity to choose for ourselves. We can do so, however, only as long as we make *conscious* choices, as long as we direct our minds and seek guidance from the right sources, the ultimate of which is the Holy Spirit.

As Billy Graham (*The Holy Spirit,* 1978) has pointed out, the Holy Spirit can only be obtained by Christian believers, and this is very much the direct result of a personal choice made by us. However, there are times when our conscious mind is seemingly no longer at work, and we find that God's Spirit takes over.

Frequently, the question has been asked whether or not actions taken under the influence of the Holy Spirit are based on objective reality. Are these actions rational? Yes, they are rational, as long as they are the kind of actions that can rationally be expected of a Christian.

In Part Three of this book, we shall discuss five rules for sound decision-making (Maultsby, *Help Yourself to Happiness,* 1975). These rules state that when something is objective, life/health preserving, goal-achieving, and allows us to feel the way we want to feel, without unacceptable conflict with others, it is self-enhancing. When three of these five rules are applicable, then most likely our thinking and behavior will be good for us. Now, these criteria are helpful suggestions only. Clearly, the first rule cannot be ignored, for if something is not objective, then we are most likely dealing with something that is not good for us.

The Holy Spirit will never force us to do anything against our will, or make us do anything that is negative or evil. To listen to the Holy Spirit does not require giving up consciousness or control. Jesus tells us, "If any man thirst, let him come unto me, and drink" (John 7:37). And, ". . . when he, the Spirit of truth, is come, he will guide you into all truth: for he shall not speak of himself; but whatsoever he shall hear, that shall he speak: and he will show you things to come"(John 16:13). The use of our minds—that is, objective thinking—is very much stressed by God throughout the Scriptures. In 1 John 4:1, 2 we read:

> Beloved, believe not every spirit, but try the spirits whether they are of God: because many false prophets are gone out into the world. Hereby know ye the Spirit of God: Every spirit that confesseth that Jesus Christ is come in the flesh is of God.

When we read on, we find that "God is love" (verse 16), and that the manifestation of God's love is to be found in our own lives:

> No man hath seen God at any time. If we love one another, God dwelleth in us, and his love is perfected in us. Hereby know we that we dwell in him, and he in us, because he hath given us of his Spirit. (1 John 4:12, 13)

It is so very obvious that we need to feed our minds with the right kind of mental and spiritual food if we are to have the joy that comes from forgiveness and goodness. When we feed our minds with garbage, we must logically expect to find unhealthy results manifested in confusion, doubts, fears, jealousy, anger, hostility, etc.

While it is not possible to live our lives without conflicts and difficulties, it is quite possible to eliminate a great deal of the misery that comes to us because of our failure to choose wisely. We may have difficulties, but this is not terrible and horrible. We can look at the entire matter from a different angle. We can say with Paul that we are troubled, but not distressed. We may be down, but already we are getting up!

Being upset is the end-result of the way we evaluate and interpret facts and events. There is no fact and there is no event that is not open to evaluation and interpretation. Praise God for many of us who have overcome some of the most severe physical, emotional, intellectual, social, and other handicaps. No, not necessarily by being healed of our afflictions. More like Job, who ". . . was perfect and upright, and one that feared God, and eschewed evil" (Job 1:1). Like Joni Eareckson (*Joni,* 1976), who tells in her most moving and inspiring autobiography "that all things work together for good to them that love God, to them who are the called according to his purpose" (Romans 8:28). Like thousands and thousands of others who were either totally healed, partially healed, or not healed, but who nevertheless can say with Paul, ". . . Most gladly therefore will I rather glory in my infirmities, that the power of Christ may rest upon me" (2 Corinthians 12:9).

Praise God that there is meaning in life and that there is meaning in death. There is meaning in health and there is meaning in affliction for the believer in Christ, because ". . . whatsoever good thing any man doeth, the same shall receive of the Lord, whether he be bond or free" (Ephesians 6:8). Truly for that purpose, and many others, we have received our minds, that we may choose to act rather than react, that we may be partakers rather than spectators, that we may be able to look above and beyond ourselves. No past, no environment, nothing of any kind can separate us from the love of God if only we reach out to him.

How sad for us if we believe that history is to blame for everything we are now or ever shall be. How tragic if we think that we are the final and total outcome of our past experiences and that we may have to live our lives in perpetual conflict and unhappiness. There is no jail cell, there are no bonds, there is no way by which our freedom of choice will come to naught as long as our minds rest in Christ. If we have no choice over our thoughts and therefore feelings, then our lives fall short from God's divine plan. He wants us to have power and dominion over this earth, and an opportunity for salvation and spiritual growth through responsible choice. We do not esteem ourselves unless we have self-esteem; we do not like, respect, or understand ourselves unless we have self-worth. We have no happiness, no joy, no comfort unless we have self-direction. It is truly a magnificent insight that we are nothing unless we partake, unless we choose to drink of the living waters and be filled to overflowing. Jesus tells us (John 7:38): "He that believeth on me, as the Scripture hath said, out of his belly shall flow rivers of living water." It is the choices we make that determine our sense of identity, our membership, our goals, our fellowship, our thoughts, our attitudes, our beliefs, our opinions, and our feelings. We can choose to do away with ". . . the old man, which is corrupt according to the deceitful lusts" (Ephesians 4:22), and we can choose to ". . . put on the new man, which after God is created in righteousness and true holiness" (Ephesians 4:24).

The devil is not going to do this for us, and God is not going to do this for us. We ourselves must choose!

Meaning is placed into our lives by the choices we make, by availing ourselves of opportunities—big or small, many or few. Happiness in life can be explained in a great number of ways (Freedman, *Happy People*, 1980). However, as a general rule, most of us will agree that we would like to survive as long and as best as we can. We like to feel good and comfortable physically and mentally, as well as spiritually. Just a moment's reflection will remind us that power, wealth, and influence will not help us one bit when it comes to being happy with ourselves. The list of powerful rulers, famous movie stars, musicians, and various idols of the general public, as well as many others in public life, who have ended their lives with drugs or some other destructive means is a lengthy one. These people eventually allowed their self-defeating thinking, feelings, and actions to destroy them totally.

It is neither wealth, nor the absence of wealth that leads to personal victory. How significant it is that all of God's gifts are free, cannot be purchased, are not for sale—and will not be denied to anyone who chooses to have them! The factors that are primarily responsible for our happiness rest with us. Helen Keller, though blind and deaf, received more sight and insight than many of us who have the use of both our eyes and ears. Joni Eareckson, though totally paralyzed, is far more productive than most of us who have no physical handicaps. The list is long of those of us who seemingly had everything and wound up leading empty, drab, miserable, or otherwise unhappy lives, and the list is long of those who in spite of very serious limitations have led and are leading fantastically happy and productive lives.

To understand what we can do with our lives begins with the insight that we experience everything within our minds and that we are the only ones who are responsible for what goes on in our minds. The good news of the gospel is only good news to us if we *acknowledge* our sins (Romans 3:23), *regret* them and change our ways (Acts 3:19), *confess* our sins (1 John 1:9), *stop* doing wrong (Isaiah 55:7), and *believe* and are *baptized* (Mark 16:16). In other words, there is no good news unless we do various things to make this good news come true in our lives. Far too many people are talking about the "good news," and erroneously believe that since Jesus came into the world to be our Savior all is well. Nothing is further from the truth. God demands that we are participators one way or the other, and that we consciously take a stand. He holds us responsible for whatever we do with all aspects of our lives, including suffering (Graham, *Till Armageddon,* 1981).

God provides every opportunity for us to choose life, fullness of life, but he does not choose for us. The good news is that our spiritual needs for forgiveness and for goodness can be filled in just a moment's notice. Our spiritual needs and our emotional, social, and physical needs can be filled as long as we choose to do so. The most important word in the English language by which we can help ourselves to spiritual, mental, and physical happiness has only two letters, namely *d-o.* We need to *do* something. How tragic that this continues to escape so many people. They spend a great deal of time listening to what it takes to make changes in their lives. Unfortunately, they often do not make any changes, for they erroneously believe that something will come from nothing.

If we are interested in helping ourselves to happiness with God's help, and rising above and beyond our troubles, then we need to understand that our feelings—happy or unhappy ones—are the result of our thoughts. Further, we need to understand that these thoughts are influenced within our mind by our past experiences, prejudices, biases, attitudes, and beliefs, but that we can learn to overrule past experiences through the process of emotional reeducation. It is when we *replace* the old with the new that we are made new creatures. Maultsby (*Help Yourself to Happiness,* 1975) emphasizes five steps in reeducative therapy, namely:

Step 1: *Intellectual insight*
    We know what to do and why.
Step 2: *Correct practice*
    The practicing of the new behavior, actually or vicariously.
Step 3: *Cognitive dissonance*
    We know something is right but feels wrong.
Step 4: *Emotional insight*
    We know something is right and it feels right.
Step 5: *Personality trait formation*
    Here we have the emotional insight plus consistent practice. Now our new behaviors become habitual—that is, natural, logical, and normal for us.

In order to overcome our troubles, we need to do more than recognize what is wrong and why. We need to be firmly committed to change, to learn new ways of thinking and feeling. The entire process is one where we move in a forward direction. We stop engaging in what has been called dysfunctional abreaction, or releasing our emotional feelings to such an extent that the whole procedure becomes countereffective. Too much talking about our problems tends to magnify them and helps us to maintain them indefinitely. On the other hand, when we reach outward, when we learn to extend ourselves beyond ourselves, then we are on the road to victory.

There is no "good news" unless we quit looking backward, unless we stop feeling so intently sorry for ourselves. After acknowledgment and regret comes restitution whenever and wherever possible. Repentance includes changing our old ways into new ways, a crossing of the bridge *and* burning it behind us.

When we are troubled, it is easy to be tempted with fear and doubt and to want to quit everything. Often when we know something is right, it will still feel wrong. The feeling portion of our brain has simply not caught up with the thinking portion of our brain. It is at times like these that we must overcome our doubts. The Scriptures warn us against being double-minded—that is, trying to have both a carnal and spiritual walk. Jesus warns us not to worry about past, present, or future concerns. He tells us that we will be fed, will be clothed, will be taken care of—period! What we are told to do is to not look back whence we came, but to look forward to where we are going: ". . . rather seek ye the kingdom of God; and all these things shall be added unto you. Fear not, little flock; for it is your Father's good pleasure to give you the kingdom" (Luke 12:31, 32). *It is at the point of cognitive dissonance that we must pay attention to God and not to our feelings.* It is at this point that we must step out in faith and move forward. We cannot serve two masters (Matthew 6:24), and we cannot give in to our feelings when we *know* that what we do is right. In James 1:8 we read that "A double-minded man is unstable in all his ways."

It is not very difficult to recognize the defiled mind, the reprobate mind, and the blinded mind. However, when we are struggling to overcome our troubles it is essential that we eliminate from our mind those self-defeating beliefs and attitudes that keep us tied to an unproductive and unhappy past. As fallible human beings, we cannot eliminate all of our self-defeating thinking and behavior; but we can get rid of enough to insure happier and more joyful lives.

The world is not the small, narrow, limited place we may have created around us. How often do we meet people who are wrapped up in minor personal problems and troubles and who fail to see major opportunities that are beckoning them. Perhaps the greatest of all deprivations is self-deprivation. Here we deny ourselves happiness, success, health, and prosperity merely because we are restricting our lives within very narrow and limiting borders of self-pity, self-blame, and other-pity. How much better for us, how much greater our immediate progress if we teach ourselves to make wise choices, become more objective, accept more responsibility, and remind ourselves that we are just as capable of being constructive as destructive, positive as negative, renewed as defiled. The output of our minds depends entirely on the input we provide.

How fortunate for us that we can learn to stop whining, crying, complaining, "awfulizing," griping, blaming, rejecting, accusing, and feeling utterly sorry for ourselves. How marvelous that our thoughts create our feelings, that we can take charge over them, that we can give executive control to the Holy Spirit. It is fantastic that we can rise above and beyond our problems and troubles, afflictions, conflicts, difficulties, disappointments, and frustrations. Thank God we can say in full knowledge and conviction that we may be troubled, but are not distressed. Our distress will disappear as long as we are willing to do the required work. God has already given us the power to do this. In the next chapters we will have a look at our emotions and how to obtain the kind of feelings we want to have.

PART THREE:

UNDERSTANDING
OUR
MIND

For as he thinketh in his heart, so is he. (Proverbs 23:7)

6   *Understanding Our Emotions*

One of the very first things we need to learn is that our emotions are made up of our *perceptions, thoughts,* and *emotive feelings.* Just have a look at the so-called ABC's of an emotion below:

A=Our Perception of an Event.
B=Our Thoughts About an Event.
C=Our Emotive Feelings as a Result of Our Thoughts.

A review of the examples that follow will quickly show us the influence of our thoughts on our feelings.

EXAMPLE #1

DEPRESSED THOUGHTS
LEAD TO DEPRESSED FEELINGS

A=Last night I went off my diet and ate a lot of harmful things.

B=I was really stupid to eat all that junk food. I will never be able to change my eating habits. I don't even know why I ate that garbage in the first place. Nobody else has such a lack of willpower. It seems that I have no choice but must stay overweight the rest of my life. I will undoubtedly get a lot worse as I get older. I don't know what to do about it, and I cannot stand being fat. Pretty soon no one will associate with me. I am a real waste.

C=I feel very depressed.

EXAMPLE #2

CALM AND HAPPY THOUGHTS
LEAD TO CALM AND HAPPY FEELINGS

A=Last night I went off my diet and ate a lot of harmful things.

B=It is true that I ate more than I wished I had. However, I am a fallible human being, and this was not as bad as last month when I ate twice as much. Actually I am pretty smart, for I did stop before all the food was gone, and I am now also realizing that it may be a good idea to buy less harmful foods in the first place. It was not garbage that I ate by any means. In fact, most of the things I ate had at least some nutrition in them. Unfortunately, most of the things I ate were high in calories. Of course, I have a choice in everything that I do. I made an erroneous choice, and I am learning from this experience. There are few, if any, people who are destined to be overweight the rest of their lives. I can learn self-enhancing eating behaviors just as well as I have learned self-defeating eating behaviors. As I get older I am actually getting smarter, and I have gained some wonderful insights even today. I know exactly what I am going to do. First of all, I am going to buy less of those things that are not good for me; and secondly, I am not going to snack during the day. People will continue to associate with me for what I am, and not for what I look like. Those people who only associate with me for my looks I may well wish to do without. I am a pretty good person to be around, contributing to others as well as learning from them. I kind of like myself. I certainly am not a waste. A human being cannot be a waste, but can be, and is, fallible!

C=I feel calm and happy.

As we quickly see from the above two examples, the events are the same in both cases. However, when we talk to ourselves in a self-defeating manner, we are going to have self-defeating feelings. It is clear that depressed thinking will lead to depressed feelings, and that calm and happy thinking will lead to calm and happy feelings.

While our feelings as a rule will be the result of our thinking, it is also true that our physical condition will greatly influence our ability to think rationally. In Part Four of this book we take a closer look at the influence of our body on our emotions. For the moment, however, we do well to remember that most of our unhappiness is caused by our well-learned self-defeating attitudes and beliefs. With our ability to make ourselves happy or unhappy we can literally make ourselves depressed under the finest circumstances, and as a result of well-learned attitudes we seemingly do not even have to think to get ourselves into trouble.

It is very important to be aware of the ABC's of emotions. Whenever we want to know what is causing our feelings, we need to go over our thoughts. If we cannot think of any thoughts, for example when we are dealing with certain well-learned attitudes, then we can merely ask ourselves what we "would have thought," given the opportunity to think about the facts or events.

There is a great amount of scientific evidence which shows that the way we respond to our perceptions will lead to the feelings we experience. For example, in the case of depression, it has been very well demonstrated (Beck, *Cognitive Therapy and the Emotional Disorders,* 1979; Brandt, *A Rational Self-Counseling Primer,* 1979; Burns, *Feeling Good,* 1980; Hauck, *Overcoming Depression,* 1976; Maultsby, *Help Yourself to Happiness,* 1975) that most depressive illness is the result of faulty thinking. The incidence of depression due to serious organic disorders is relatively small. However, extensive drug use, more appropriately called legalized drug abuse, is enormous.

In the United States, billions of pills are swallowed each year to give us either a lift or to bring us down. Graedon (*The People's Pharmacy,* 1980) points out that we spend about half a billion dollars for about sixty million prescriptions of Valium alone! Now it is well-known that Valium is generally not used for organic disorders, but rather to help us cope with the so-called stress and strain of daily life. According to Graedon, we use more than 120 million prescriptions every year for mood-altering drugs, *exclusive* of the number of prescriptions written for patients who are hospitalized.

While it is undoubtedly true that there are some cases where the use of any drug may be beneficial, the number of cases where mood-altering drugs are indicated are insignificant compared to the number of prescriptions that are being written. Unfortunately many people receive tranquilizers for such physical symptoms as dizziness, tachycardia, shakiness, etc., which very often are caused by such things as glucose imbalance. The taking of tranquilizers may temporarily mask the problem, not necessarily because of its effect on the central nervous system, but rather its effect on the endocrine system.

Reeducative therapy or self-counseling is all that most of us need to overcome our drug addictions—from Valium to alcohol, from nicotine to caffeine. We are a nation of sugar, caffeine, nicotine, alcohol, Valium, and other drug junkies! Some of us are so enwrapped in the doping-up process that our minds are not drug-free long enough to be used in a self-enhancing manner.

Since depression is one of the more serious common problems we encounter on a day-to-day basis (the most common problem is anger with ourselves, others, and our environment) and for which usually erroneous treatment is instituted, we will need to spend a few moments looking at this phenomenon. Depression has been widely discussed by a great many people. It has been thoroughly researched, and yet there remains a very great deal of confusion and misunderstanding. We need to realize that it is quite normal to have feelings of occasional sadness as a result of some serious loss, failure, disappointment, or frustration.

In depressive illness, however, there is such a great change in our usual behavior that it is very noticeable, not only by us but also by others in our environment. Our grief seems endless; the things we used to like and were able to do we no longer like and/or cannot do. We are simply not functioning well. We go around with a gloomy sadness, feel isolated, extremely lonely, and often apathetic. Agitation, tearfulness, forgetfulness, hopelessness, sadness, and despair are but some of the more common manifestations of depression.

Many things have been tried for the treatment of depression, but when people suffer from depression caused by fallacious thinking, all the drug therapy, shock therapy, or in-depth psychoanalysis, etc. will be of no avail! In fact, it has already been shown that about half of the depressions will disappear in time *without any treatment whatsoever.* The reasons for this are clear if we understand the ABC's of emotions. Since we are always communicating with ourselves, it is the eventual change in our self-communication (due to many factors) which leads to the so-called spontaneous remission of many depressions. Of course, depressions caused or aggravated by physical disorders—e.g., hypoglycemia—start to disappear when proper physical treatment has been initiated (see Part Four).

While excellent research is going on in psychobiology, and interesting things have been found to possibly implicate certain brain chemicals as the cause of depression, we are still left with the overwhelming day-to-day evidence (and our practical experiences) that psychological depressions are usually caused by self-defeating thinking, and usually respond to self-enhancing thinking. Since about 75 percent (or more) of all depressions are of a psychological nature, we are well advised to pay attention to the ABC's of emotions.

The ABC's of emotions tell us that most depressions are primarily thinking disorders (Beck, *Cognitive Therapy and the Emotional Disorders,* 1979; Brandt, *A Rational Self-Counseling Primer,* 1979; Burns, *Feeling Good,* 1980; Hauck, *Overcoming Depression,* 1976; LaHaye, *How to Win over Depression,*

1974; Maultsby, *Help Yourself to Happiness,* 1975), and the correct therapeutic approach is to work on our thinking. Of course, there are the obvious depressions which are the result of some very serious loss—for example, through the death of a loved one. In that case, it is still true that it is our opinion, our interpretation of what that loss means to us that leads to the depression; however, experience has shown that most people want and need some time to go through a grief process.

For Christians, however, even here we might expect some noticeable differences when compared to non-Christians. Death is not the end for the Christian, but rather a whole new beginning (2 Corinthians 5:8). And for those of us who are left behind, "the sufferings of this present time are not worthy to be compared with the glory which shall be revealed in us" (Romans 8:18).

The kind of depressive problems that many people suffer from are not necessarily caused by some *recent* serious loss or grave disappointment. I have counseled many people who had suffered from depressions for many years, in some cases even decades! What these people had been doing was keeping an old depression well and alive by a mental continuation of problems that were since long gone. For example, I often find bitterness and resentment toward parents who are no longer alive, or who are no longer in contact with the depressed person.

Dr. Aaron Beck has emphasized that often depressions come about, and are maintained, by misinterpretation of facts and events, and by negative interpretations. He has warned that whenever our thinking departs too much from rational and realistic thinking, we may well suffer from a negative self-concept and come to seriously overstate and overstress our problems. Although our depressive feelings are the result of disturbances in our thinking, often a vicious cycle starts in which our unhappy feelings give rise to further unhappy thoughts.

Dr. Maxie C. Maultsby, Jr. agrees with Dr. Beck and others that depressive thinking will lead to depressive feelings, and he emphasizes that the neocortex precedes the limbic system, and that our behavior normally follows a pattern of *thinking, feelings,* and *actions.* Dr. Paul Hauck stresses that the three most common reasons for all nonorganic depressions are to be found in *self-blame, self-pity,* and *other-pity.* If we are self-blamers, we have a tendency to believe that we are totally bad. One of the sad things is that many Christians who believe that Jesus died for them on the cross continue to wallow in self-blame, where more appropriately they could spend that time thanking God and praising him for setting them free from *all* of their burdens, including guilt.

Of course, it is important for us to be appropriately sorry for our sins, but it is also essential that we *do* something about them: make restitution whenever and wherever possible, accept God's forgiveness, and determine not to do destructive things again. God wants us to go for total victory—indeed never to stay down, but always to get up that one more time, so that we may reach the mountaintop.

Those of us who blame ourselves excessively, who do not wish to accept God's forgiveness, see ourselves as superhuman beings (again see Hauck). We insist and demand that we ought to have been perfect, and miss the entire concept of fallibility. God knows that we are not perfect. He created us. God is fully aware of our ignorance, stupidity, and disturbances. He has provided an answer for all those things. He has provided an opportunity for us to choose joy over misery.

God is not looking for a world filled with self-blamers, who go about with negative attitudes and sour faces, and whose contribution to mankind is that they wallow in self-blame. He expects us to walk in faith, hope, and love, in commitment and loyalty to the things we received, so that we are new creatures in Jesus Christ. We read in 2 Corinthians 5:17, ". . . if any man be in Christ, he is a new creature: old things are passed away; behold, all things are become new." If there is still any doubt in our mind, then we best read the following verses (18-21), so that we may learn that we are indeed *reconciled* to God.

And all things are of God, who hath reconciled us to himself by Jesus Christ, and hath given to us the ministry of reconciliation; to wit, that God was in Christ, reconciling the world unto himself, not imputing their trespasses unto them; and hath committed unto us the word of reconciliation. Now then we are ambassadors for Christ, as though God did beseech you by us: we pray you in Christ's stead, be ye reconciled to God. For he hath made him to be sin for us, who knew no sin; that we might be made the righteousness of God in him.

Are we blaming ourselves when God no longer blames us? Are we carrying on in despair when we can walk in hope? As self-blamers, we are seeing ourselves as unworthy; yet God deems us worthy enough to have his Son die for us. As self-blamers, we see ourselves as giant mistakes floundering around on earth; but does God make mistakes?

We blame ourselves for our lack of intelligence, the absence of one thing or another, and our self-esteem is zero. Does God see us as worthless? Would he have sent his Son to die for us? The Scriptures tell us that "God so loved the world, that he gave his only begotten Son, that whosoever believeth in him should not perish, but have everlasting life" (John 3:16). Are we to go through life as self-blamers? God tells us that ". . . he hath chosen us in him before the foundation of the world, that we should be holy and without blame before him in love" (Ephesians 1:4). Are we to go through life with sad faces, disliking ourselves? God tells us that when we walk with him, we will be filled with joy (Psalm 16:11).

Now it is not only *self-blame* that will lead to depressions, for we have already mentioned *self-pity* and *other-pity.* When we go around feeling very sorry for ourselves, it is usually because we believe that others are to blame and that we have little or no control over our emotions. We tend to think that whatever is happening to us is horrible and terrible, even catastrophic. We believe that few people suffer as much as we do, that the world is not fair, and that we are victims of a cruel, unfair, or sick environment. We feel singled out!

Frequently there is no basis in fact for all the things that we perceive are happening "to" us. Even if there was objective evidence that we were undergoing serious difficulties, it would still be what we told ourselves that would lead to the feelings of self-pity. It is only when we *tell ourselves* we are in despair that we begin to feel that way. God warns us not to talk to ourselves in that manner, so that we do not become depressed. In

2 Corinthians 4:8, 9 we read, "We are troubled on every side, yet not distressed; we are perplexed, but not in despair; persecuted, but not forsaken; cast down, but not destroyed." When we perceive our situation (A) as troublesome and serious (B), then we will undoubtedly feel concerned (C). However when we perceive our situation (A) as distressing, despairing, and destroying (B), then we will undoubtedly feel depressed (C).

In the case of *other-pity,* we find that we have overconcern rather than concern for others. When we are overly concerned, we have a tendency to become less and less effective. Other-pity is usually so painful and unhealthy that it becomes nonconstructive. Perhaps this is why we are told not to ". . . (suffer) . . . as a busybody in other men's matters" (1 Peter 4:15). For if we are busybodies we are meddlers, paying more attention to others than is good for them or for ourselves. The ABC's of emotions are very much at work here. When we are *telling* (B) ourselves all of the horrible, terrible, awful, disastrous things that others are experiencing, then *we* are going to feel (C) depressed. Whether the actual fact or event (A) was based on objective reality or not does not matter.

Since it is difficult enough for us to be objective about our own perceptions, it is obviously even more difficult to be objective about the perceptions of others. As a result, we often grossly misinterpret what is going on in the lives of other people. Worse, many of us begin to believe that it is necessary to become personally upset over their disturbances. While few, if any, of us would consider breaking our legs because so many other people seem to have broken legs, we consider it our duty to destroy our minds because so many others are doing it. Few of us would consider willingly contracting some serious disease because our children suffer from it; yet it seems easy for us to indulge in the emotional disturbances of our loved ones. Unfortunately, other-pity does not make big problems smaller. It makes small ones big, and big ones bigger.

It is important that we do not misunderstand what has been said here. It is important to help one another. In Galatians 6:2 we read, "Bear ye one another's burdens, and so fulfill the law of Christ." Only by loving others can we do the will of God. We are charged, when we are strong, ". . . to bear the infirmities of the weak, and not to please ourselves" (Romans 15:1). Clearly we need and want to help others. However, it is obvious that we can only carry those who have no legs when we have legs ourselves. We can only console others when we are consolable. We can only reduce conflict when we are not ourselves too angry or upset.

Out of love we need to identify with others, and when we are able (capable, healthy, etc.) then we need to carry the burdens of others. We must not, however, become part of the problem, and leave that much more for others to do. Of course, God will come to our rescue, for he has identified with all of our suffering and he is, in fact, the only one who can do so. God is omnipresent, omniscient, and omnipotent. We are incapable of redeeming ourselves, let alone others. While we must strengthen our bodies and minds, and be ready to help others, we must never allow ourselves to be destroyed mentally or physically. The exception would be to voluntarily sacrifice our life for another person's life, as we read in John 15:13: "Greater love hath no man than this, that a man lay down his life for his friends."

As we are dealing with our problems and serious difficulties, we need to steadfastly look to God. Our perceptions of certain facts and events in our life (A) may be unchanged, but God will help us to change our negative self-talk (B) and lead us to victory, so that once again we will feel calm, if not happy (C). When we are analyzing our self-talk (our attitudes, beliefs, opinions, etc.) we shall do well if we remember Isaiah 63:9: "In all their affliction he was afflicted, and the angel of his presence saved them: in his love and in his pity he redeemed them; and he bare them, and carried them all the days of old." What we cannot do, God has already done. Praise God!

However, we can do a great deal ourselves. To help ourselves and others we need to walk in the Holy Spirit, let our light shine (yes, with a happy face!), and teach others how to find that true and lasting source of our greatest joy. The only way I know in which we can express our concern for others is through applied love. The only way we can do it is by being capable: that is to be as healthy as possible—physically, mentally, and spiritually. It is a responsibility we have to ourselves, to others, and to God. It is unfortunate that many Christians often fail to take care of this responsibility.

In this chapter we have discussed the importance of understanding our emotions. It is important to know that an emotion is more than just a feeling we have. When we better understand the three component parts of an emotion, we may learn to have more of the emotions we want. Hopefully, we thoroughly understand that our thinking is the all-important ingredient.

Produce your cause, saith the Lord; bring forth your strong reasons. (Isaiah 41:21)

7 Making Sound Decisions

In order to make sound decisions we need to know what we mean by "sound decisions." Surely what one person considers a sound decision may be considered a very unwise decision by others. As Christians we have many things in common. Even when it comes to decision-making we can rest assured that there are certain decisions we will all agree upon as being sound for all of us. For example, no Christian will doubt that it is a sound decision to accept Christ, to repent from our sins, or to live in the Holy Spirit. Yet, when it comes to our day-to-day affairs there will be serious differences as to what is a sound decision. Moreover, what may be a sound decision for us this morning may not necessarily be a sound decision this afternoon. Let us look at this phenomenon.

Most of us know that sound decisions can only be made by those who are of a sound mind—i.e., the kind of mind that has average functioning intelligence, that is free of incapacitating illness, and free of intoxicating drugs. The most advantageous way for us to make decisions requires the use of logic and searching for principles that will help us to make objective inferences. Clearly it is important to avoid as many fallacies in our reasoning as we can. We need to be extremely careful not to come to conclusions that do not follow from objective reality. We need to learn not to make hasty generalizations, and to delay our reactions long enough to evaluate adequately whatever facts and events we are dealing with at the moment (Johnson, *People in Quandaries,* 1946). It has been found essential to be as relaxed and calm as possible when it comes to sound decision-making. Interestingly, the latter will reinforce the former, and vice versa!

If there is one concept where much confusion and serious problems arise, it is in the concept of "allness." Christians need to be acutely aware that many of the charges made against them, such as being too absolutistic, dogmatic, and perfectionistic, are not without foundation. However, there are no human beings in the world who do not have some absolutes, who do not follow some dogmatic rules, and who do not show some perfectionistic tendencies. Those who shout the most often show definite manifestations of absolutism, dogmatism, and perfectionism. Some of our behavioral scientists are on overly zealous missions in which they declare (in very absolutistic and dogmatic ways) that there is "absolutely" no truth to religion, that there is "absolutely" no God, and that the "only" way to be "completely" adjusted is to follow them! It is interesting to note that some of these specialists often exhibit, especially in their own lives, serious social and emotional difficulties. Nevertheless, we do well to recognize that our thinking (beliefs, attitudes, etc.) can only be objective to the extent of our genetic endowment, our "imperfect" knowledge, and our "limited" experiences, in a very "subjective" world—subjective to the extent that little of the world is known to even the most scholarly and best-informed scientists. We are fallible human beings; we are not God!

We need not apologize for our absolute belief in a loving and living God who has set definite standards and rules if we desire to become perfect. The desire for perfection, for goodness and forgiveness is a noble, wholesome, very rational desire.

The making of sound decisions is essential to happiness and success in our lives. We are well advised to evaluate frequently the roads we take on our life's journey. The absolutism of the Christian who gives sovereignty to a loving and living God who is omniscient, omnipotent, and omnipresent is a far cry from the absolutism displayed by authoritarians and totalitarians who seek to enforce their worldly powers over suffering humanity. The absolutism of the Christian is based on faith and is the expression of a sincere belief in the positive power of absolute love.

There is no arbitrariness in the Christian's choice; it is not a blind choice; it is not based on blind faith. We become Christians only by choice, only after we realize that one way is preferable over another. The mistaken idea that many of our zealous opponents have about us is that we are irrational. However, this is very inaccurate. We are rational, for we are engaged in making self-enhancing choices. We are rational, for we are living our lives with the least possible amount of conflict, with the greatest possible amount of love. We are rational, for we want to survive as long as possible, with the greatest hope and least frustration.

We are also busy in liberating ourselves from the bonds of negative and destructive forces. We recognize the destructiveness of hate, hostility, anger, jealousy, greed, selfishness, worries, anxieties, resentfulness, and hundreds of other manifestations that are the direct result of a lack of faith, hope, and love. The lack of self-respect, lack of good reputation, and lack of self-sufficiency that is so typical of a world without Christ can be transformed into positive self-evaluations and a peace with Christ that transcends all forms of security, whether economic or personal or social.

Now to return to the concept of "allness." This concept which is expressed in such terms as all, always, never, ever, everybody, nobody, forever, at all, at no time, evermore, etc., is far more important to us in the day-to-day minor decision-making process than in major matters of faith and religion. It is the absolutism that we apply to ourselves in such things as believing that we will "never" be able to change, that "all" people are dishonest, that "nobody" will ever marry us, etc., which we need to watch.

To be dogmatic means to have firm beliefs. There is nothing wrong when these beliefs are based on objective reality and have proven themselves to be of value. We may choose to have certain dogmas—that is, to follow certain creeds or teachings.

It is not wise to do so, however, unless we have rationally thought about these beliefs.

Many of us are suffering from intolerance, closed-mindedness, arrogance, and opinions that are the result of blindly following something we have heard or seen. For sound decision-making we need to have open minds, and we need to be willing to listen and to evaluate. It is important that we learn to distinguish between fact and opinion, between fact and desire, between fact and presumption, between fact and prejudice or bias. Indeed, we need to learn to become more objective and less subjective.

We will not be able to do this very well when we erroneously believe that we are better than others. It is very easy to believe mistakenly that we "should" not have any weakness, etc. The truth of the matter is that we need to strive for perfection, but will not be able to attain this on earth for the many reasons that we have already discussed in this book and which are summed up in the concept of fallibility.

For sound decision-making we need first of all to learn to *stop* and *think*. Only when we stop and think will we have a chance to evaluate facts and events, and analyze our self-talk about them. We need to develop a good habit: namely, the habit of learning to question our opinions, beliefs, attitudes, etc.

From the discussion on the ABC's of emotions, we have already learned that our emotions are made up of our perceptions, thoughts, and emotive feelings. It is important to realize that our emotions, positive or negative, will often interfere with, and even prevent, our reasoning from logical principles. We are also bound by the limitations of our genetic makeup and our past experiences.

In order to learn to make sound decisions, it is necessary to closely follow the principles of logic. We need to watch for minimizing as well as for magnifying, for understating as well as for exaggerating. We must not jump to conclusions, make hasty generalizations, or categorize people. It is best to stop and think, and question the validity and reliability of our thinking, so that we may determine if it is based on objective reality.

If our thinking is based on objective reality—that is, true

facts—then we are fulfilling the first requirement of sound decision-making! In order to help us determine if something is based on objective reality, we may wish to ask ourselves if a camera, taking a picture unencumbered by opinions, attitudes, and beliefs, would have registered the same impressions (Maultsby, *Help Yourself to Happiness,* 1975).

The question that all of us have to answer is whether or not something is good for us. Something is "good" for us if it is based on reasonable criteria for decision-making. To know if something is good for us, we can use Dr. Maultsby's five criteria for sound decision-making.

If we are like most human beings, we have a strong desire to survive and to feel good, comfortable, and happy. When our thinking or behavior goes contrary to our strong desires for happy survival, then they are of a self-defeating nature. However, in most life situations it is useful to have some additional guidance. What is good for one person may not be good for another. What is good for us today may not be good for us tomorrow. When three of the following five rules apply, our behavior or thinking most likely is rational:

1. It is objective.
2. It protects our life or health.
3. It helps us to achieve our goals.
4. It allows us to feel the way we want to feel.
5. It keeps us out of the trouble we don't want.

Those five rules seem very simple, and to most of us are merely common sense. Unless we commit these rules to our memory and consciously apply them in our daily life, however, we will not make much progress with sound decision-making and self-counseling.

Most of us wish to lead our lives as fully and happily as we possibly can. We will search for ways and means to improve our life situation and to change those things that are undesirable or unpleasant for us. Of course, there are circumstances beyond our control. In the Scriptures we read that we are "troubled on every side, yet not distressed; perplexed, but not in despair" (2 Corinthians 4:8, 9). This is a very important point to remember. For when we are in a difficult and unhappy situation, it is highly unlikely that we are going to be happy about it. However, as reasonable human beings we will do everything necessary to accept those things that cannot be changed as calmly as is humanly possible.

While we are already suffering because of an unpleasant condition over which we have no control, why should we add unnecessarily to our suffering? It is far better for us to remember the ABC's of emotions and the five rules for sound decision-making and to accept the fact that the world is an orderly place, where everything happens according to strict laws. While we may undergo annoying, disagreeable, unpleasant, yes, unhappy experiences, there is still no doubt that everything happens in accordance with strict laws.

If we do our very best but still fail in something, then we should fail, for there are certain prerequisites missing to insure our success. Failing at something, however, does not make us failures. We already know that we can be no more and no less than fallible human beings. Even with the very best system of decision-making, even with the finest of educations, even with the hardest work, we will remain fallible.

One very sound decision we may wish to make is to stop being overly demanding and to quit insisting on self-defeating shoulds, musts, and oughts. God loves us as fallible human beings. God accepts us with our failures and mistakes. God reminds us that in the long run everything will work out right for us, as long as we love him (Romans 8:28).

We are under the voluntarily chosen law of love. There is no sound reason for us to whine, demand, and insist that we must be Number One in all things. To believe that we have to be Number One, that we cannot fail, that we must always be in control, and that our value as human beings depends upon worldly success, will lead to feelings of depression, despair, rejection, and worthlessness.

In order to successfully overcome many of our day-to-day problems, we need to become far more objective. An excellent systematic approach to problem-solving is found in the so-called Objective Self-Analysis (Maultsby, *Help Yourself to Happiness,* 1975). This is a simple, yet effective approach to problem-solving and verifying of reactions to facts and events. The Objective Self-Analysis (OSA) is based on the three parts that make up an emotion—namely the *perception* of an event (A), the *self-talk* about an event (B), and the *emotive feelings* that result from the self-talk (C).

And ye shall know the truth, and the truth shall make you free.
(John 8:32)

8   The Objective Self-Analysis

There are a number of ways by which we can learn to analyze our behavior, feelings, and thinking. However, one of the most effective and efficient ways to do this has been found in Dr. Maultsby's (*Help Yourself to Happiness,* 1975) Rational Self-Analysis (RSA), which we will refer to in this chapter as Objective Self-Analysis (OSA). The OSA is preferably done in writing, especially when we first start out. One of the many advantages of the OSA is that it is based on the three parts of an emotion—namely, the *facts and events,* our *thinking* about the facts and events, and our *emotional responses* to our thinking about the facts and events (see Chapter 6).

In order for us to challenge whether or not our self-talk is objective, we simply use the five rules for sound decision-making. The following is a simplified version of the OSA format.

A = EVENT
B = SELF-TALK
C = FEELINGS
D = QUESTIONING/CHALLENGING
E = NEW FEELINGS/THE WAY WE WANT TO FEEL (IF APPLICABLE)

OSA SAMPLE # 1

A. FACTS AND EVENTS. Last night I went off my diet and ate a lot of harmful things.

B. SELF-TALK. I was really stupid to eat all that junk food. I will never be able to change my eating habits. I don't even know why I ate that garbage in the first place. Nobody else has such a lack of willpower. It seems that I have no choice but must stay overweight the rest of my life. It will undoubtedly get a lot worse as I get older. I don't know what to do about it and cannot stand being fat. Pretty soon no one will even associate with me. I am a real waste.

C. FEELINGS. I feel very depressed.

D. CHALLENGING/QUESTIONING. It is true that I ate a lot more than I wished I had. However, I am a fallible human being, and this was not as bad as last month, when I ate twice as much. Actually, I am pretty smart, for I did stop long before all the food was gone, and I am now also realizing that it may be a good idea to buy less harmful foods in the first place. It was not garbage that I ate by any means. In fact, most of the things I ate had at least some nutrition in them. Unfortunately, most of the things I ate were high in calories. Of course, I have a choice in everything that I do. Last night I made an erroneous choice, and I am learning from this experience. There are few, if any, people who are destined to be overweight for the rest of their lives. I can learn self-enhancing eating behaviors just as well as I have learned self-defeating eating behaviors. As I get older, I am actually getting smarter, and I have gained some wonderful insights even today! I know exactly what I am going to do. First of all, I am going to buy less of those things that are not good for me, and secondly, I am not going to snack during the day. People will continue to associate with me for what I am and not for what I look like. Those people who only associate with me for my looks I may well wish to do without. Whatever, I am a pretty good person to be around, contributing to others as well as being willing to learn from them. I kind of like myself. I certainly am not a waste. Human beings cannot be wastes; all that we can be is fallible.

E. NEW FEELINGS. I feel happy and calm.

NOTE: We could have made good use of the five rules for sound decision-making by applying them one by one to each of the statements of the self-talk section (B). We would have found that most of these statements were not true, not health-preserving, not goal-achieving, not allowing us to feel the way we would like to feel. Some of the statements in the self-talk section contained "allness" terms such as "never" and "no one," which upon evaluation will prove to be irrational and unrealistic.

OSA SAMPLE #2

EVENT SIDE	CHALLENGE SIDE
A. FACTS AND EVENTS	Da. CHALLENGE TO A
B. SELF-TALK	Db. CHALLENGE TO B
C. FEELINGS	E. CHALLENGE TO C

By placing the event side and challenge side next to each other, it is easier for us to use the five rules for sound decision-making. In order to challenge A, it is very important to be scrupulously honest with ourselves. Dr. Maultsby recommends that we ask ourselves if a recording device—for instance, an audiovisual tape recording—would have recorded the event exactly as we described it. Sometimes, of course, we cannot do this—for instance, when we are dealing with feelings.

When is a good time for us to do an Objective Self-Analysis? The answer to that question is simple. A good time to do an OSA is any time we wish to check on our emotive feelings, be they positive or negative. In most instances, however, we will probably do an OSA on an emotive feeling that is undesirable to us. It is best when we do our OSA as quickly after an event as possible. The reason for this is that when we wait, we are likely to forget some of the details. Also, by doing the OSA when we are most upset, we will get help when we need it the most.

As we can see from the examples, we list the facts or the events, as we remember them, in Section A. We then list our thoughts, beliefs, attitudes, opinions, etc., in Section B, followed by a statement of how we felt, or how we are now feeling, in Section C. The best way to do an OSA is first to list the fact or event in Section A, followed by a description of our feelings in Section C, and only then to write our thoughts in Section B.

After we have done these three things, we are ready to ask ourselves some questions and to challenge our perceptions and thoughts. We do this by writing in the Da section the facts and events as they would have been registered by a recording device, such as a TV camera. It is quite possible that this camera will come up with the same information that we already have in our A section. This simply means that the facts and events as we remembered them were based on objective reality.

When we are dealing with a feeling, we cannot do a camera check. We may, for instance, have the following A statement: "I felt happy when I saw her." If that is an accurate statement, then our challenge section will have the same statement: "I felt happy when I saw her." Alternately, we may wish to rewrite our statement as follows: "I saw her." Then in the Da section we would also write "I saw her," or simply write out the word "True." In the C section we would then write that we felt "happy."

It is the purpose of the D sections not only to challenge the facts and events, to be sure that they are based on objective reality, but also to challenge the self-talk with the five rules for sound-decision making as follows:

Is this thought *factual?*
Does this thought *lead me to protect my life?*
Does this thought *get me to my goals most quickly?*
Does this thought *help me to feel the way I want to feel?*
Does this thought *keep me out of the trouble I don't want?*

When we use these five rules for every thought in our self-talk

(B) section we will, through objective challenge and debate, arrive at a new more objective alternative (Db).

In the E section we describe our new feelings, how we feel now, or would have felt had we followed objective thinking. We also list the new actions we would now take, or would have taken had we followed objective thinking. In the F section we describe our anticipated objective perceptions to some future fact or event, as well as our desired objective thoughts, feelings, and actions. This section is of the greatest importance when we start to work on learning how to change our thinking and behavior as described in the next chapter. For additional instructions we can refer to the Objective Self-Analysis format below.

INSTRUCTIONS:
1. Copy this format on a blank piece of paper. Fill in the letters A, B, C, Da, Db, etc.
2. Under A we fill in the facts and/or events as best we remember and as concise as possible.
3. Under C we list how we feel (or felt) and what we are doing (or did).
4. Now we fill in the B section and list some of our prevalent thoughts about the facts/events. This includes beliefs, attitudes, etc.
5. We challenge A by asking if it is true/objective. We ask if an audio-video camera would have recorded the same facts/ events.
6. We challenge every statement in the B section with the five rules for sound decision-making and list them in Db.
7. We describe in the F section our future desired thoughts, feelings, and actions to anticipated facts/events.
NOTE: The Objective Self-Analysis deals with past, present, and future behavior. It is an extremely powerful device which helps us to learn from the past and thus to ensure a happier future.

THE OBJECTIVE SELF-ANALYSIS

A. FACTS AND EVENTS (PERCEPTIONS)	Da. OBJECTIVE VERIFICATION AND CORRECTION OF PERCEPTIONS	Fa. FUTURE FACTS AND EVENTS (ANTICIPATED PERCEPTIONS)
Undisputed	Disputed	Programmed
B. SELF-TALK (THOUGHTS, BELIEFS, ATTITUDES, OPINIONS, ETC.) 1. 2. 3. 4.	Db. OBJECTIVE CHALLENGES 1. 2. 3. 4.	Fb. FUTURE DESIRED SELF-TALK (OBJECTIVE ALTERNATIVES TO B AND Db) 1. 2. 3. 4.
C. (1) FEELINGS (2) ACTIONS (BEHAVIOR)	E. (1) NEW FEELINGS (2) NEW ACTIONS (BEHAVIOR)	Fc. (1) FUTURE DESIRED FEELINGS (2) FUTURE DESIRED ACTIONS (BEHAVIOR)
Past	Present	Future
Objectification		Visualization

From this chapter we have hopefully learned that the *best* way to analyze our perceptions, thoughts, and emotive feelings is to do so in writing, using a logical sequence. Please remember that our emotive feelings come about as follows:

A. We perceive something.
B. We have thoughts about it.
C. We have emotive feelings about it.

This provides us with the anatomy of an emotion. It tells us how the emotion came about. If we are satisfied with our feelings, we do nothing else. If we are not satisfied, we sit down and do an OSA. This means making sure that:

Our perceptions are factual.
Our thoughts are objective.
Our feelings are the ones we want.

We have now learned a scientific way of recognizing self-defeating or other unwanted personal opinions, attitudes, and/ or beliefs. This is not enough, however. If we are interested in learning new behaviors and having new feelings, we have to *practice* those behaviors and feelings. As in most things, it is the *doing* that counts. Insight is only one step in the process of reeducative counseling. Actually there are five steps: namely, intellectual insight, correct practice, cognitive dissonance, emotional insight, and personality trait formation as the result of consistently doing that which is both right to do and feels right as well

Of all the steps, none is more important than learning to *do* the new behaviors we are looking for. In order to learn our new behaviors quickly and painlessly, we can make excellent use of systematic mental image training. The next chapter will tell us more about that!

Therefore if any man be in Christ, he is a new creature: old things are passed away; behold all things are become new. (2 Corinthians 5:17)

9 Learning New Self-Enhancing Behavior

Of all the chapters in this book, none is more important than this one. After all, what good does it do if we know all about our behavior but cannot make necessary self-enhancing changes? From the start it should be clear that we *can* learn new self-enhancing behavior. We *can* be happy. We *can* do away with addictions—of any kind!

Contrary to what we have been told, and contrary to what we are telling ourselves, it is neither difficult nor impossible to learn new behavior. Of course it *is* difficult or impossible to change if we tell ourselves so and then believe it. There is only one thing that stands between us and positive behavior changes, and that is lack of faith. Neither wishing nor demanding, neither doubting nor fearing has any place in our thinking if we are going to change our behavior.

We can change because God has promised we can have all which we need. In John 15:7 he tells us, "If ye abide in me, and my words abide in you, ye shall ask what ye will, and it shall be done unto you." How is this done? By asking and then doubting, making excuses, and rejecting? By asking and not meaning what we are saying? Jesus says, "For by thy words thou shalt be justified, and by thy words thou shalt be condemned" (Matthew 12:37). Certainly it is important to choose our words wisely. However, there is more. In Mark 11:23 we find this: "For verily I say unto you, That whosoever shall say to this mountain, Be thou removed, and be thou cast into the sea; and shall not doubt in his heart, but shall believe that those things which he saith shall come to pass; he shall have whatsoever he saith." Do we see that it involves actually choosing and speaking the right kinds of words? However, *choosing* and *saying* words is not going to help us unless we also *believe* in the very words that we speak. We must choose, say, and believe (Capps, *The Tongue: A Creative Force,* 1977).

We are the end-product of words. When we change our words, we will change our behavior and change our future. When we change our words, we will move from darkness to light. How simple, how incredibly miraculous! In Hebrews 4:12 we read, "For the word of God is quick, and powerful, and sharper than any two-edged sword, piercing even to the dividing asunder of the soul and spirit, and of the joints and marrow, and is a discerner of the thoughts of the heart." The Word of God is omnipotent, omniscient, omnipresent, and everlasting. Everything can be done with God's power, and we have been given the awesome responsibility to use that power here on earth. Yes, we *are* in a position to use God's power. In Proverbs 18:21 we read, "Death and life are in the power of the tongue: and they that love it shall eat the fruit thereof." Praise God that we can use our minds to think, choose, and speak.

There is no doubt that God wants us to exercise *responsible* choice. He tells us in Deuteronomy 30:19, "I call heaven and earth to record this day against you, that I have set before you life and death, blessing and cursing: therefore choose life, that both thy and thy seed may live." It is clear that God wants us to choose wisely, and that he has provided us with everything that is needed to do so. Through the power of divine thought, we can conquer everything that needs to be conquered in accordance with the will of God. We must not misunderstand God's will by negatively preempting him, by assuming that he wants us to be poor, sick, hungry, or lonely. God wants us *to choose* between "blessing and cursing," and he wants us to have the kind of faith that will give us "whatsoever" we say. This is what the Scriptures say; this is what God teaches us. Interestingly, this is also what many modern behavioral scientists have discovered.

Beth Brown (1971) in her marvelous book, *Your Words Are Your Magic Power,* so very aptly explains that a "word is not merely a word. It is a unit of power that generates your life." I doubt if she could have known at that time of the research of Dr. John Diamond (*Your Body Doesn't Lie,* 1980) and others in the field of behavioral kinesiology. However, his findings and the findings of others are quite clear: we can strengthen and/or weaken our body responses not only by stress, posture, and specific foods, but also by our emotions—that is, *by the thoughts we use.* Dr. Diamond found that thoughts of hatred reduce our life-energy and that thoughts of love increase our life-energy. That research and a great deal of other research in psychosomatic medicine and in behavior therapy, and my own work (*A Rational Self-Counseling Primer,* 1979) all underscore that we shall be justified or condemned by our words (Matthew 12:37).

The Scriptures emphasize that our thoughts lead to feelings and actions. Evil thoughts lead to evil actions, and good thoughts lead to good actions. Thoughts are made up of words. We can do ourselves a great service by paying more attention to the words we use.

Kenneth Hagin (*Words,* 1979) as a young boy was very seriously ill and declared incurable. However, he acted on Mark 11:23, 24, and believed that he would be healed. He acknowledged receipt of the healing, and the healing came about. Kenneth Hagin, Bill Basansky (*The Land of Milk and Honey,* 1977), Ruth Carter Stapleton (*The Gift of Inner Healing,* 1976), and many others who received personal healing entered into healing ministries of faith. In a previous chapter I have already discussed that not everyone will be healed. Objective reality has shown us that some people are and some people are not. However, we must be careful not to preempt God.

As I said in the beginning of this chapter, it is neither difficult nor impossible for us to learn new behavior. The great obstacle is doubt, the enemy of our faith and the friend of Satan. In this chapter we will look at some *proven* facts about how people can and do change. This chapter is not based on theory, but practical experience. I know for a fact that we can change self-defeating thinking, feelings, and actions into self-enhancing thinking, feelings, and actions. Norman Vincent Peale (*The Positive Principle Today,* 1976) calls it the "alteration" principle. I know for a fact that with God there are neither helpless nor hopeless cases, and that he has given us the power to help ourselves. The good news is that positive behavior change is relatively simple, as long as we have a sincere desire to do the required work. For change to take place, we must meet a few simple prerequisites.

One prerequisite is learning to recognize self-defeating beliefs and attitudes. For example, the general irrational philosophy that we cannot change is reflected in the self-defeating belief, "You cannot teach an old dog new tricks." While that is a somewhat inaccurate belief about dogs, it is an even more inaccurate one about human beings. Scientists and laymen alike are all too often confusing animal behavior with human behavior. The truth is that regardless of age, human beings can and do change their behavior. Age is not the primary ingredient for positive behavior change in human beings. The primary ingredient is a strong desire, kindled by an even stronger faith.

While the first obstacle to learning self-enhancing behavior is doubt, the second obstacle is lack of skills. To learn skills we need incentives and opportunities. Our environment is important to the extent that it may or may not provide us with incentives and opportunities from which to choose. Clearly we must look for opportunities to enrich our environments. It is self-evident that the more opportunities we have for positive physical, mental, and spiritual stimulation, the greater our chances will be for participating in them.

Many of us have been fortunate enough in childhood, adolescence, and/or adulthood to have been blessed with stimulating as well as wholesome environments. However, we need to be aware that even if we lacked such an environment in the past, this does not mean that we cannot set out to find and/or create a better environment. The important truth is that our past does not have to determine our future. With the help of God, we can learn to surround ourselves with the kind of people and things that will encourage, stimulate, inspire, and help us.

To change the behavior of others we often use *positive rein-*

forcement. This principle can also be applied to ourselves. We can learn to regularly *reward ourselves.* One way by which we do this is to set not only long-range, but also medium- and short-range goals. Each time we reach a goal, we already experience the intrinsic reward of feeling good. We can potentiate this by extrinsic rewards as well. At each step we can reward ourselves with encouragement (it is not a sign of mental illness to speak encouragingly to ourselves!) and with some small physical reward—e.g., buying something we have wanted for a long time, going for a visit, or taking time off work. The important thing to remember is that we are making history, that we are learning something new. Success breeds success, and once we master one step of our program, we are more inclined to go ahead and learn the next one.

In this book we have a step-by-step program. The lessons are so arranged that we need to study each chapter in the order that they are presented. For example, it is very important that we thoroughly understand the ABC's of emotions before we learn the five rules for sound decision-making and the Objective Self-Analysis. When we go slowly and regularly through all this, we *are* learning new behavior.

We can also learn to increase or even to create our motivation. We are not only talking about motivation (needs) for survival, but, rather the motivation to rise above and beyond survival problems. The motivation or desire we are talking about is of a higher level than survival, and deals with an all-embracing mental and spiritual happiness that transcends our everyday cares and concerns. Motivation is a strong desire to get something, or to get away from something, or both. Motivation, like self-control, does not fall out of the sky, and we are not born with it. Motivation is no more and no less than learned behavior. If we do not have enough of it, we simply decide that we are going to increase it. The secret ingredient to increasing our desires will also be found in words. If we continue to talk in the old way, by saying such things as, "I wish I had more motivation," or "I wish I had as much motivation as Mary Lou," then we are unlikely to succeed. On the other hand, if we tell ourselves, "I am more motivated every day," or, "I thank God for my power of self-motivation," then we are going to increase our motivation. We will feel instantaneously better, and feeling better we will be more likely to do something constructive. The more positive our self-talk, the more we shall be filled with life-energy (Diamond, *Your Body Doesn't Lie,* 1980) and the more we shall succeed. That's why more and more is given to those who already have. Motivation is a decision, for we can literally make up our minds to desire something or other. Thank God that we do not have to wait for others to give us motivation. What a long wait it would be!

Obviously motivation is something for which we work. Nothing comes from nothing. We need to think before we leap; however, thinking by itself will not bring success. The secret ingredient for increasing our motivation is to be found in words *and* action. Success or failure hinges on a very small word: to *do* or not to *do*. The Lord promises us that we shall find him if we seek him with all our heart (Jeremiah 29:13). It is interesting to note that we have to "seek" (to do), and that this holds true throughout the Scriptures. There is only good news *if we do something.* We are reminded to come, to drink, to seek, to knock, to search, to ask, to choose, to believe, to accept, to abstain, to love. All verbs! Praise God that we have a guaranteed promise that action will beget action. Love begets love! If we are not willing to help ourselves, then we can forget about learning the kind of behavior that we would like to have. Whether we take the thirty-second solution and step out in faith, accepting God's promises and claiming victory, or decide to make slow and gradual changes in our lives, in either case we have to *do* something.

As long as we continue to confuse ourselves with such irrational beliefs (actually they are outright lies!) that we cannot stop smoking, drinking, or hating, then we will not be able to change that behavior in the least. God has made that very clear to us. Remember, we are justified or condemned by our words. We shall have what we say. That includes failure and holding on to our destructive habits. There is not one person on earth who cannot stop smoking, drinking, or hating. Why then do we have such great difficulties in "trying"? God never said, "If you try to believe, you can move that mountain," or, "If you try to believe, you will be healed." No, God makes it clear that we either do or do not believe! Trying is a long ways removed from doing. In fact, trying may well be a convenient excuse for double-mindedness. The Scriptures warn us that "A double-minded man is unstable in all his ways" (James 1:8). There is no such thing as quitting tobacco and also wanting to enjoy the artificial "energy" lift, or the "pacifier effect." We cannot have our cake and eat it too. For example, we want to be free from some problem, but we are unwilling to give up our bowling night to go to group counseling. Are we anxious because we are doing illegal, immoral, or unhealthy things, and yet are not willing to give them up? When we are double-minded, all so-called trying is fruitless.

Every second, every minute, every hour, every day, 365 days a year, people are changing their lives from defeat to victory. Only those of us without reasoning faculties fail to see that we can and do change. When we have a strong *desire,* have *faith,* and are *committed,* then we always change. When a Christian says he cannot change, he denies God's power and truth. When God tells us to "choose" between blessing and suffering (Deuteronomy 30:19), how can we sanely say that we are condemned to ruin our bodies and health, to sell our birthright to happiness?

It is generally accepted that we need insight, motivation, and opportunity if we wish to learn new behaviors. Fortunately most of us have access to all of these things. Most of us who conscientiously follow the principles of *objectification* and *visualization* as described in this book can and will change self-defeating behavior into self-enhancing behavior!

In the Scriptures we read that we must "put on the new man" (Ephesians 4:24; Colossians 3:10). There is nothing that says "*try* to put on the new man." No changes will be made unless we make them. Being exposed to knowledge will not turn us into knowledgeable people; it takes more than that. We can memorize this book from beginning to end and be totally unchanged. Only when we step out in faith will our faith come to life. We are participators. We are the drivers who will have to make the changes if there are going to be any.

However, we will not make any changes unless we are first aware that we have choices. We will not translate awareness into reality unless we have a strong desire for one thing over another, and *believe* that we can and will attain our goal. It is clear that we will learn new behavior as long as we fulfill certain prerequisites. On the negative side, we may find such motivating factors as pain, frustration, dissatisfaction, boredom, and unhappiness. On the positive side, we may find such motivating factors as faith, hope, and love.

In the preceding paragraphs we have talked about the power of faith and how we can have, often instantaneously, what we ask for in faith. However, we need to understand that there is more than one way by which we can help ourselves to health and happiness. Both natural and supernatural positive behavior change is good, and both gradual and instantaneous positive behavior change is possible. In this book, the main emphasis is on gradually learning (and relearning) self-enhancing thinking, feeling, and behaving. The latter system is usually preferred by most people.

As said before, this book is so designed that it needs to be studied from beginning to end, and no chapter should be omitted if we are to get the full benefits. Part Three, "Understanding Our Mind," especially needs to be studied page by page. This particular part of the book also requires that we do a daily amount of homework. After we thoroughly comprehend the ABC's of emotions, and have become proficient in applying the five rules for sound decision-making to our day-to-day affairs, then we need to spend some time writing Objective Self-Analyses (OSA's), so that our thinking, feelings, and actions become more and more self-enhancing. We can greatly speed up the process of emotional reeducation by learning to become proficient in self-enhancing mental imagery (Maultsby, *Help Yourself to Happiness,* 1975), or Objective Visualization Training (OVT). The latter sounds somewhat forbidding; however, it is very easy and something that all of us are doing to some extent already.

In order to make gradual changes in our behavior, we need to have practice in the new behavior we desire. We need to practice until our new behavior becomes habitual. Dr. Mary Greene, in *A Guide to Rational Weight Control* (Brandt, 1980), explains habit formation as follows: "The more you engage in a particular behavior, the more likely it is that you will engage in that behavior again! In other words, habits are formed by doing the same thing over and over again. It seems as though habits create patterns in our brain similar to the way rivers are formed. The more water that flows through a river, the deeper and wider it becomes. If you want the water of a river to flow to a different place, it is necessary to dig a canal and divert the flow of water. In the same manner, if you do not like a habit you have, then it is necessary to deliberately refuse to practice it, and to practice doing something else instead. Eventually a river will erode away if no water flows down its path. In the same manner, your old habits will die out if you replace them with new ones."

It is clear that when we practice our new behavior long enough, this behavior will become habitual. In fact, once this happens, the reeducation process has been completed. The trouble that most of us have is that we usually cannot get enough safe practice to learn our desired new behaviors. The answer to that difficulty is found in practicing in our mind. In order to do Objective Visualization Training we create or form pictures in our mind of a situation (fact/event) in which we act out our future desired behavior. By seeing ourselves in that new situation, we mentally practice thinking, feeling, and acting in our desired objective way.

The very best way to become proficient in Objective Visualization Training (OVT) is to make it an integral part of our Objective Self-Analysis (OSA). Ideally, we first complete an OSA and then follow this with visualization exercises. This will help us to ensure that we are practicing in a self-enhancing manner. Visualization exercises are essential to reeducative therapy. It is most important to remember that OVT is not only objective, but also essentially positive and realistic.

Most of us participate in many visualization exercises that are subjective, negative, and/or unrealistic. For example, if we are overeating on a daily basis, and yet practice seeing ourselves as slim and trim, then we are merely wasting our time and practicing illusions. That would be dangerous nonsense. There is nothing dangerous, however, about OVT. It is not a game, and it is not phony.

Objective Visualization Training (OVT) helps us to practice

in our minds the desired thoughts, feelings, and behavior that we have described in our Objective Self-Analysis.

Effective OVT requires a scenario, just as in the production of a film. This scenario or script is the only guideline we follow when we do our mental imagery. We can do OVT on any OSA we have completed. If we know that we want to do OVT on something, then we first complete an OSA. Once we have completed our Objective Self-Analysis, we can prepare our scenario. The first part of the scenario is based on the Fa section of the OSA. Here we objectively describe a *future anticipated situation* (based on information derived from our Da Section). Being as factual and concise as possible, and using the first tense, we explain what we see and hear. The following is an example of OVT on making ourselves less anxious when we are going to give a speech at our local church:

I am entering the church and walking to the front to find my place in the speakers' row of the church, facing the entire congregation. The pastor is present and sits down on my left, and the choir director takes a seat to my right. The members of the choir are sitting behind me. There are many guests and visitors in the church, and several people have come to listen to my talk.

The next part of the OVT scenario (Fb) includes all of *the future desired self-talk* we have selected. For example, we can say:

It is a wonderful opportunity to serve God as a speaker this morning. It does not matter how many people are in church or how many guests and visitors are there. It does not matter if I make some errors or not. It is not possible to be perfect, and it is neither possible nor necessary to be loved by everyone. No one in the congregation can make me upset. Rather than making myself upset about what people think, I am concentrating on serving God and enjoying the opportunity to the fullest. I refuse to be anxious or upset. What people think and say cannot hurt me. I can only upset myself, and that is both a waste of time and self-defeating. I chose to speak. I enjoy the view, enjoy my thoughts, and enjoy the opportunity to serve God.

The final part of the scenario, taken from the Fc section in our Objective Self-Analysis, tells us what *we do* in the actual situation. This is the action script we might see before our eyes, and we hear ourselves say:

> I am now sitting comfortably in the speakers' row. I enjoy the full view of the church and enjoy seeing so many new faces in the congregation. I am calmly waiting for my turn to speak, and when my turn comes I eagerly begin my talk, starting off by saying, "I am really glad to have this opportunity." I remain calm and happy throughout my talk.

After we have prepared our scenario in writing, we may also decide to record it on a tape and listen to it until such time that we have committed the scenario to our memory. Such a tape-recording will be very short, perhaps only a few minutes in duration. Actually we can make a series of scenarios on one tape and practice as much as we wish. Listening to our voice on the tape-recorder in combination with seeing ourselves doing all those self-enhancing things we so much desire becomes a powerful learning experience.

By now we will understand that this vicarious practice (practicing in our minds) is synonymous with watching a movie. We are watching a movie on the screen of our mind. In fact, we are watching a movie starring ourselves and flooding our mind with information that is going to give us all the new behavior we desire. It is important to realize that we are not pretending and we are not playing games. We are very seriously learning new self-enhancing behaviors.

The best way to do OVT is three times a day, for a period of ten minutes as follows:

- We practice as much as possible at the same times in the same location. We relax ourselves as much as we can, perhaps utilizing some breathing exercise. We find a comfortable and quiet place. With our eyes closed, we are now ready to go over our scenario.

- The scenario is ideally taken from the F section of a well-done OSA.

- In our scenario, we see ourselves in the situation (Fa) described in our OSA, and we go over and over the self-enhancing self-talk (Fb), and our new behavior and emotive feelings (Fc).

- As an additional incentive, we schedule our OVT before breakfast and before lunch. We may refuse to have lunch until such time that we have completed the OVT. Finally, we do OVT immediately before falling asleep.

Objective Visualization Training is one of the safest, sanest, yet most powerful and efficient methods to learn new behaviors. We only change to the extent of our personal involvement. We change to the extent that we have faith and hope. We must see, believe, and feel. We must not depend on our feelings, but follow after fact. We must also not misunderstand the importance of feelings. We have been promised the positive feelings of love, joy, and peace when we walk in the Holy Spirit. When these fruits are absent, then we might wonder what else is absent?

The importance of OVT is highlighted by the fact that no therapeutic change whatsoever can take place unless we project ourselves into the future and see change. The more precisely we practice in our minds what we are after, the more precisely shall we get those things. In order to do our OSA's and OVT's well, we need to be sure that we take the time to do them correctly. We need to arrange our environments as much in our favor as we possibly can.

We also need to make sure that we get enough sleep, fresh air, exercise, recreation, relaxation, and proper nutrition. We need to learn that we cannot separate body, mind, and soul. Plato, the Greek philosopher, said more than 2,000 years ago that it was one of the most serious mistakes of his time that physicians separated the body from the soul. There is no doubt that it is even a more serious problem today. We need to make optimum use of our surroundings and of our bodies, mind, and spirit.

Objective Visualization Training is the answer to most of our problems, even ones over which we seemingly have no control. Situations that are beyond our control and which we cannot

LEARNING NEW
SELF-ENHANCING BEHAVIOR

THE NATURAL APPROACH*	
GOALS	**STEPS**
1. Intellectual insight.	1. ABC's of emotions.
2. New behavior.	2. Rules for sound decision-making.
3. Dissonance of thinking and feeling.	3. Objective Self-Analysis.
4. Emotional insight.	4. Objective Visualization Training (vicarious practice).
5. Personality trait formation.	5. Consistent actual practice.
THE SUPERNATURAL APPROACH:*	
GOALS	**STEPS**
1. Awareness.	1. God's Word.
2. Hope.	2. Faith.
3. Decision.	3. Say and believe.
4. Desire.	4. See and feel.
5. Acceptance (inner healing/physical healing).	5. Walk in the Holy Spirit.

*Christian reeducative therapy makes use of both the natural and the supernatural approach to learning new behavior. In either case, the Scriptures are the foundation and we apply our faith to the fullest extent, so that victory may be achieved by obtaining a "renewed mind" in Jesus Christ.

change can still be dealt with in a constructive manner. All our mental movies may not have a happy ending, but all of them can have a constructive and worthwhile lesson. We are the ones who will determine how we are going to feel about whatever has happened, is happening, or will happen.

Let's summarize a few points about Objective Visualization Training (OVT). Mental imagery can be used to our advantage or disadvantage. One of the most advantageous ways to use our mental projective power is in an objective as well as positive and realistic way. OVT essentially consists of practicing in our minds the way we wish to think, feel, and act in the future. It is a safe, efficient, and effective system that requires our undivided attention for about ten minutes, three times daily. Correctly done, OVT provides us with the mental practice for things we will soon do in actual practice.

On the following page is an outline of the steps and goals involved in the learning of new self-enhancing behavior. This outline summarizes many of the things we have discussed in this chapter. Please note that in Christian reeducative therapy and self-counseling we can freely choose to use the natural and/or supernatural approach to learning. In either case, however, the Scriptures are the foundation on which we build. It is only by following the Lord that we can obtain the desires of our heart (Psalm 37:4).

PART FOUR

A SOUND MIND
IN A
SOUND BODY

I beseech you therefore, brethren, by the mercies of God, that ye present your bodies a living sacrifice, holy, acceptable unto God, which is your reasonable service. (Romans 12:1)

10 Emotional Problems May Have a Physical Basis

One of the more serious mistakes we frequently make is to overlook the important part that our body plays in our mental health. When our body chemistry is disturbed, then frequently our minds will also be disturbed, and it will become increasingly difficult to walk in the Holy Spirit. Considering what is at stake, it is truly amazing how lightheartedly we deal with our health. While this book emphasizes reeducative therapy and self-counseling, it must be realized that we cannot reach our goals unless we pay very close attention to the interrelationship of body, mind, and spirit.

As Christians we are charged with the responsibility to be as healthy as possible, and to stay alive as long as possible. We are told that our body is "the temple of the Holy Ghost" (1 Corinthians 6:19) and a "living sacrifice" (Romans 12:1), in which "Christ shall be magnified" (Philippians 1:20). Our responsibility is very clear; however, our actions frequently belie our understanding of it!

It is clear that we need to respect our bodies, if for no other reason than that we are created in God's image (Genesis 1:26, 27), and that our body is the abode of the Holy Spirit. However, there are many more reasons as well. We need to respect, accept, and understand as much about our bodies as we possibly can, so that we may fully appreciate God's creation. Only through respect, acceptance, understanding, loyalty, and faithfulness can we come to love ourselves as we have been commanded to do. God wants us to love ourselves, as he wants us to love him and others.

Of course, even if there was no relationship whatsoever between the health of our body and mind, we would still want to take care of our bodies for optimum physical health. As Christians, we should desire to look and feel at our very best at all times to the glory of God. Our responsibility goes far beyond looking and feeling good physically, for we first need to look and feel good spiritually.

Over the past years we have continued to learn a great deal about psychosomatic illness. We have come to know that our minds directly affect the functioning of our bodies. We realize that we may become very ill because of worry, anxiety, fear, doubt, hatred, jealousy, anger, and greed. The further we stray away from the guidance of the Holy Spirit, the more our troubles multiply. Just as our minds can influence our bodies to the point of physical illness, so can our bodies influence our minds to the point of emotional illness.

Negative body influences may arise from organic disease, trauma, toxic substances, and many other situations; however, the most prevalent seems to be improper nutrition. We may truly speak of psychosomatogenic and somatopsychogenic disorders. The disturbing stimuli may be found in our environment, bodies, and/or our minds.

Most of us are well aware that negative emotions may lead to physical illness; however, we often fail to realize that negative emotions may arise from perceptual-cognitive and/or proprioceptive stimuli. Please do not think that this goes contrary to what we have been discussing in the earlier chapters of this book. The truth remains that our minds are in charge of our bodies, for our thoughts lead to feelings and actions. The process, however, is not always clear-cut. Our emotions, paradoxically, are both simple and complex.

Undoubtedly most of us, most of the time, will be able to refer to the ABC's of emotions, the five rules for sound decision-making, and the Objective Self-Analysis and find that our particular brand of thinking has led to our particular brand of emotional experiences. Yet, we must remember that our brain (mind) is an electrochemical computer which is completely tied in with our physical, mental, and spiritual life. The close inter-relationship of our body, mind, and spirit is manifest in most of the things we do, or fail to do. When we have an unfulfilled spiritual need for goodness and/or forgiveness, then this will be reflected in our emotional and/or physical health. If we hate, we deplete both our physical life energy *and* upset our emotional equilibrium (Diamond, *Your Body Doesn't Lie,* 1980).

Dr. Frederick R. Stearns (*Anger,* 1972) has reported on a number of well-documented studies which have shown that negative emotional reactions to external stimuli are often seriously augmented and magnified by proprioceptive stimuli. Both our external and internal environments play a vital role in our physical, mental, and spiritual health. Glandular, allergic, and other physical conditions have a tremendous effect on our emotive behavior.

Still, most of our unhappiness is of our own making, due to the self-defeating way in which we think. Ideally we learn to zero in on both internal and external inputs. For example, even when we have a well-diagnosed organic difficulty (such as depression due to insufficient lithium), then we must still realize that we are no different than others. We are still subject to perceptual-cognitive factors and/or additional proprioceptive factors, such as a lack of certain vitamins, disturbed glucose, or calcium-phosphorus levels in the blood. Stressful stimuli—whatever their origin—need to be identified and dealt with.

Living in today's world is increasingly difficult. Regardless of where we live, we are exposed to a good deal of stress in our environment. For one thing, there is no place to hide from the air, water, and soil pollution. All of us live in toxic environments. In the United States we are under the constant attack of carbon monoxide, ozone, nitrogen dioxide, lead, cadmium, strontium 90, and many other dangerous substances. We are assaulted daily by poisons in our food supply. Chemical substances such as potassium and sodium nitrates have been shown to be "powerful cancer causing agents" (Winter, *A Consumer's Dictionary of Food Additives,* 1978).

Hundreds of dangerous additives are in our processed food supply, and the U.S. government has not been able to control this situation and cannot in any way guarantee to protect our health. We are the only ones who can do this—to some extent at least. We can find alternate natural food supplies and stay away from processed foods. Not only is our food supply poisoned, but so is the air we breathe and the water we drink. These are excessive stresses, and we need to have very rational minds to effectively combat the dangers and reduce the risks. Under no circumstances can we afford to increase the problem by using dangerous sprays, food additives, nicotine, caffeine, etc. We need to be watchful that we do not participate in harmful things. If we do not make major changes in our lifestyle, away from the unnatural and back to a more natural way of life, we will continue to have excessive physical as well as emotional difficulties.

Poisonous substances, noxious fumes, and many other stressful irritants are an obstacle to our desire to present our "bodies a living sacrifice, holy, acceptable unto God . . ." (Romans 12:1).

The time has come to carefully and consciously take the necessary steps to reduce and/or to eliminate excessive physical and mental stress, and begin to improve our presently impoverished health. As one of the richest nations on earth, we have been poor stewards. We rank after many far poorer nations in overall health and mortality rates. Self-help groups will hopefully become microunits where healthful living will be taught and mutual assistance will be provided. This can be done in much the same manner that food cooperatives are helping us to help one another to a better and healthier life. Specialized self-help groups are also very important. I had the pleasure to attend an allergy self-help group in Great Britain. This group, under the guidance of Mrs. Heather Hyne, greatly impressed me with the successful manner in which they had been able to help themselves. In this group there were people who had valiantly battled for years with such physical and emotional problems as depressions, migraines, etc. Most of them had seen a number of specialists, all in vain. However, by becoming aware of the symptoms of food and other allergies, and by learning how to isolate the responsible allergens, these people are now leading happier, healthier, and more productive lives. Actually it is in the United States that most of the original work in the field of food and other allergies has been done.

While it is true that many of our emotional problems may have a physical basis, this does not mean that we dare neglect perceptual-cognitive factors. In fact, our thinking is virtually always involved regardless of where the original stimuli originated. As I have stated several times, most of us suffer from emotional problems because of the erroneous ways in which we think. Nevertheless, it is essential that we understand the influence of our bodies on our minds. A great number of problems, such as anxiety, depression, hyperkinesis, nervous tension, mental confusion, and many others, are often the result, for example, of chemical allergies (MacKarness, *Chemical Victims,* 1980), and/or poor nutrition (Airola, *How to Get Well,* 1974; Fredericks, *Low Blood Sugar and You,* 1969; Sheinkin and Schachter, *Food, Mind & Mood,* 1980; Somekh, *The Complete Guide to Children's Allergies,* 1980; Smith, *Feed Your Kids Right,* 1979).

It is important to realize that our present knowledge about the influence of the body on the mind has become quite extensive thanks to the work of experts in the field of physiology, biochemistry, medicine, psychology, dentistry, and many other fields, including anthropology. A number of excellent books are now on the market for use by the general public by such experts as Marshall Mandell, M.D.; Arthur F. Cocoa, M.D.; David Sheinkin, M.D. and Michael Schachter, M.D.; Lendon Smith, M.D.; Emile Somekh, M.D.; Paavola Airola, Ph.D.; Harvey M. Ross, M.D.; John Diamond, M.D.; Carlton Fredericks, Ph.D.; Richard MacKarness, M.D.; Melvin Page, D.D.S.; E. M. Abrahamson, M.D.; Alan Nittler, M.D.; Roger Williams, M.D.; Joe Nicholas, M.D.; and many, many others. I list these names because all too frequently we meet people who believe (as many powerful commercial interests would like them to believe) that some faddist or fanatic has artificially created a menacing disorder just to scare us. The story is quite different. Many dedicated medical and other experts in this country and abroad have independently discovered many of the dangerous abuses of modern technology which seriously endanger our health.

The interrelationship between body and mind (Diamond, *Your Body Doesn't Lie,* 1980), and vice versa (Benson, *The Mind/Body Effect,* 1980) has clearly been established, and we can no longer approach emotional problems without considering both somatopsychogenic and psychosomatic factors. Of course, this highlights once again the need for a thorough physical examination by a competent physician. Yet, even with such an examination we need to be mindful of our personal responsibility in matters of health and healing. A physician can only help the healing process along. Only God and nature can cure our bodies. However, we ourselves play a most vital role in this entire matter, with our attitudes and beliefs.

Many of our emotional problems may be caused and/or influenced by bacterial or viral disease, or by trauma. More frequently, however, our emotional, mental, and/or behavioral problems are caused/influenced by a combination of (1) self-defeating thinking, (2) excessive stress, and/or (3) sin.

While self-defeating thinking usually plays the predominant part, it is always necessary to look at all areas of our physical, mental, and spiritual lives. Failure to do so will make it increasingly difficult for us to survive. The primary mechanism that God has given to us by which we may help ourselves to greater health and happiness is our mind. It is as essential as ever before to make the best possible use of our minds. We need to realize that much of our so-called progress in our modern civilization is really retrogression. For we are not always moving to greater health and happiness, but moving backward to illness and sorrow. Modern technology and human greed are responsible for many seriously damaging stress situations on the human body. Perhaps the most common, as well as the most devious one, is the damage that is being done by the use of sugar to our entire civilization. For example, the abuse of sugar has led to an epidemic of hypoglycemia, or low blood sugar, and many other sugar-related problems. Refined or processed sugar is one of the more destructive commonly abused substances around. Sugar, the all-time great enemy of our health, is the great and powerful friend of commercial interests that feed us billions of pounds of the stuff in virtually everything that we buy, bringing in billions of dollars of profits.

Manufacturers, advertising experts, and various others have successfully managed to create a secondary need to use more and more of a substance that has zero nutritional value and causes havoc with our life-regulating endocrine system. It may first appear to be incredible to hundreds of thousands of victims, but their heart palpitations, sudden panic reactions, feelings of terror, depressions, anger, sudden fears, bouts of anxiety, dizziness, headaches, shakes, etc., are often directly caused by nothing else but the use of refined sugar products (many others suffer similar problems due to allergens, toxic substances in food and water supply, etc.). Sugar is a truly wicked substance, for it comes with a sweetness that even many of its victims (diabetics, hypoglycemics, etc.) will continue to use, knowing that it will cause them severe harm, perhaps even their death.

Why is so little known about the sucrose disaster? Because the facts are not known? No, the facts are known; however, we are getting exactly what we are asking for. We have the secondary need, and we demand that it be satisfied. Nothing will change in the production and sale of such harmful products as refined sugar, alcohol, caffeine, nicotine, etc. until we, the consumers, quit buying this dangerous junk. Please note that another major danger is lurking just around the corner with the increased sales of sugar substitutes (in spite of warning labels!). Most sugar substitutes are also dangerous products and are increasing our secondary need for too much sweetness. Artificial sweeteners (saccharin, sodium saccharin, sodium cyclamate, potassium cyclamate, etc.) are synthetic drugs. These chemicals are just one more irritant that we can well do without! The use of artificial sweeteners *increases* our needs for sweets and *decreases* the sensitivity of our taste buds for natural sweetness. This deadly combination is certain to make us even more dependent on increasing amounts of artificial sweetness. In addition, the safety of the artificial sweeteners remains in doubt (Page, *Your Body Is Your Best Doctor*, 1972).

In this book we cannot discuss all the various stress factors at length; however, because of its prominence, we will look somewhat closer at the problems surrounding the use of refined sugar. It has been shown that refined sugar is implicated in a host of degenerative diseases as well as mental and behavioral problems, all of which are associated with a condition commonly known as hypoglycemia or low blood sugar.

HYPOGLYCEMIA I
WHAT, WHY, WHERE, AND HOW

It is not possible for us to have good physical and/or mental health without proper body chemistry. The latter, in turn, is not possible without a properly functioning endocrine system. To understand anything at all about hypoglycemia (low blood sugar) or hyperglycemia (high blood sugar), we need to know something about the glandular structure that is responsible for the chemical control of our bodies. This structure, the so-called endocrine system, consists of small ductless glands which release various powerful chemicals directly into our bloodstream.

Either overactivity or underactivity of our endocrine system will lead to serious problems. Whenever there is a serious disturbance in the regulation of important elements in our blood such as sugar, calcium, or phosphorus, then our health is in jeopardy. For example, the reason millions of people suffer from hypoglycemia is due to the fact that their endocrine systems are malfunctioning. Our endocrine system (chemical factories, consisting of ductless glands) produce a few dozen different chemical substances (called hormones) which literally determine how we function. Our endocrine glands are closely interrelated—if one is out of order, it affects the entire system, and consequently our entire body.

Our glands are very powerful determiners—together with our nervous system—of all our physical activities and functions. Our brain (mind) can be seen as a supersensitive electro-chemical computer. Whenever there is a serious electrical or chemical disturbance in our brain, this will be demonstrated in our behavior. Hormones have the specific function of urging on other actions within our body. In fact, they provide impulses for other organs and glands to regulate our health and well-being. All of our glands are interrelated with one another, and when one is over- or underactive this will be compensated for by a so-called opposite gland, so that chemical balance may be maintained in our body. For example, overactivity of our pancreas will lead to underactivity of our anterior pituitary gland. When the pancreas malfunctions, then the adrenal glands will respond with the release of an increased amount of adrenalin.

The *pituitary* gland, located at the base of our brain, is known as the master gland because its hormones direct the functioning of the other glands such as the ovaries, testes, thyroid, and adrenal glands. Other glands are the pineal gland and of course the thymus gland which recently has been described as the regulator of body energy (Diamond, *Your Body Doesn't Lie,* 1980).

The *adrenal* glands, located at the top of our kidneys, have an inner portion, called the medulla, which secretes adrenalin, and an outer layer called the cortex, which releases several hormones that regulate the rate by which we use sugar in our bodies. Without our adrenal glands we could not live, for, among many other things, they maintain our essential sodium and electrolyte balance and play a major part in the manufacture of glycogen in the liver.

The next chemical factory we want to look at is the *pancreas.* This gland has stolen the limelight in virutally all discussions about hypoglycemia because of its function in raising and lowering our blood sugar levels. The pancreas, found just below the stomach, is not only an endocrine, but also an exocrine gland. The pancreas produces two hormones—namely insulin, which lowers blood sugar levels, and glucagon, which increases our blood sugar levels. Glucagon is especially important to the liver, where it activates glucose. When our blood sugar goes down, the secretion of glucagon increases and the secretion of insulin decreases, thus maintaining a necessary balance. Insulin is produced by the well-known islands of Langerhans of the pancreas. These groups of cells are very sensitive to sugar, which leads to their secretion of insulin. Without insulin the cells in our bodies cannot use sugar, and we would die.

When we think about the functions of our adrenal glands or pancreas, it quickly becomes apparent that they play a major role in hypoglycemia. In fact, low blood sugar is just as related to the low functioning of the adrenal glands (known as hypoadrenocorticism) as it is to the increased functioning of the pancreas (known as hyperinsulinism). As was pointed out before, we all know that our body energy is derived primarily from sugar. It is no wonder that the largest internal organ in our body (the liver) and several of our chemical factories (endocrine glands) are charged with the responsibility of regulating the manufacture, storage, and use of sugar.

The liver plays a very important role in regulating our blood sugar levels, because it stores both sugar and glycogen (sugar which the liver has converted into liver-starch), and then converts the glycogen back into sugar again. In addition, the liver can manufacture *protein* from carbohydrates or fat, or it can manufacture *carbohydrate* from fat or protein. What is more, the liver can also manufacture and store *fat,* from carbohydrate or protein which it can release in the form of fatty acids. These are then burned as energy by the cells of the body.

The digestive system and the endocrine system are obviously created to handle unprocessed, natural foods, so that the stomach, intestines, liver, gall bladder, pancreas, and adrenal glands can all play their very specific interdependent roles. This holds true in particular for the manufacture of sugar in our bodies. Whenever we eat refined sugar products, we bypass the mechanisms that are created to regulate the manufacture, storage, and use of sugar, thus leading to serious disturbances in our endocrine system and our overall physical and mental health.

The reason why so many people have hypoglycemia is due to the fact that they consume an excessive amount of refined carbohydrates. Our endocrine system simply cannot effectively handle this, and consequently we undergo a very rapid rise in blood sugar levels. This leads to excessive insulin levels, which in turn upsets other endocrine glands such as the adrenal and anterior pituitary gland, and also affects other organs such as the liver, and disturbs our central nervous system.

Because of the rapid rise in blood sugar caused by refined carbohydrates, and in particular sugar and sugar products, our endocrine system responds by depressing our blood sugar levels below normal. The use of refined carbohydrates simply leads to an overreaction by our endocrine system. Once our blood sugar level has fallen low enough, the liver will respond to hormonal signals and release some of the stored glycogen, which it first converts into sugar.

When we regularly use refined carbohydrates, we are repeating the rapid rise and fall of our blood sugar levels. Eventually this will lead to damage of our adrenal glands and impairs the functioning of other glands. The more we abuse our endocrine system this way, the weaker the system gets and eventually, in addition to hypoglycemia, we may also get diabetes. The reason why so many people use candy and other sweets as well as caffeine, nicotine, and alcohol is because their blood sugar levels are totally disturbed. What most of us do not recognize is that as long as we use these products, they will destroy our endocrine systems more and more. Thus, the need for alcohol, sugar, coffee, and cigarettes will continue to increase.

Earlier we mentioned that emotional problems may have a physical basis, and when we see how stress affects our endocrine system, we can better appreciate that fact. It is not at all surprising that low blood sugar affects millions and millions of people in the United States. It is noteworthy that the overweight population in this country exceeds over 100 million people, and we can observe two things. First, the overweight suffer from the same problem as the hypoglycemics—namely, the misuse of refined carbohydrates, and consequently a seriously disturbed metabolism. Secondly, we find that there are a disproportionately large number of overweight people who suffer from hypoglycemia and hyperglycemia (diabetes). We also know that metabolic disorders can be inherited, and when the present trend continues, we will have increasing numbers of children that will be born with metabolic disorders. It is also noteworthy that diabetes and other degenerative diseases are virtually unknown among those people who do not use refined carbohydrates. The fact that metabolic disorders may be inherited does not mean that we cannot create our own metabolic disorders, for we are doing it every day. Furthermore, it also does not mean that our bodies do not have regenerative abilities. We can learn to compensate greatly for many of our physical defects.

As for the incidence of hypoglycemia, I have been giving a questionnaire to students in my college classes which indicated that about 10 percent of this allegedly healthy population sample reported numerous physical and mental difficulties which were indicative of hypoglycemia. Virtually every one of those students who followed up with physical examination and a Glucose Tolerance Test (GTT) have hypoglycemia. In my work with overweight people over the past few years, I have found that up to 50 percent of the overweight suffer from a number of symptoms indicative of hypoglycemia, and again virtually everyone who followed up with a physical examination and GTT was found to have fasting or reactive hypoglycemia. This finding, although alarming, is not startling, for when we look at the primary causes of overweight it would be miraculous to find that most of the overweight could have a normal metabolism. In my travels in Europe and the United States, I have observed that eating natural fat is probably not a primary factor in overweight (MacKarness, *Eat Fat and Grow Slim,* 1975). But without a question there is a relationship with the junk food that is increasingly being consumed in this country (Brandt, *A Guide to Rational Weight Control,* 1980).

Hypoglycemia is a stress disorder which comes about as a result of seriously disturbing our endocrine system with (1) harmful products, (2) overwork, (3) poor nutrition, and (4) excessive negative emotions. Consequently, when we deal with disorders of this type we need to make more than only dietary changes. We need to undergo a total transformation. This book hopes to help us with that goal. A transformed life is what we are after. When we have a renewed mind and walk with the Lord, then it seems that we would also want to have a healthful life-style.

We cannot overstress the importance of looking at all the areas of our life, be they physical, mental, or spiritual. We need to learn to pay attention to detail and ensure that we do not go against our own dearest goals. For example, when we are committed to exclude as many additives from our food as possible and spend time and effort on this, yet continue to buy dangerous cosmetics (e.g., certain lipsticks, body sprays, etc.) with scores of additives that are not good for us, then we are clearly wasting our time.

It seems silly to refuse to smoke, yet not to refuse to sit in smoke-filled rooms, or not to refuse to use dangerous chemical sprays in our homes and kitchens. It is more than self-defeating to refuse a can of beer, but to gladly accept a cola drink. Most of the damage that we are doing to our bodies is due to lack of knowledge and wisdom. God tells us that we should ask him for wisdom and he will give it to us. In this area too we need to ask for his help. Certainly as long as we are not only ruining our own health, but also the health of the children that have been entrusted to us, there is something wrong. For example, children are rarely permitted by us to drink "real" coffee, yet we gladly give those poor children a cup of cocoa (or chocolate bars!), which contains far more caffeine than coffee. An eight-ounce cup of cocoa contains from 50-250 milligrams of caffeine. A regular cup of coffee contains about 100 milligrams of caffeine. We really do harm our children with cocoa, chocolate, and cola drinks (30-65 milligrams of caffeine, plus other dangerous substances like sugar). Should we continue to give them chocolate milk, candy, and other junk food? Must we continue to feed them those quick-to-serve, easy-to-make cereals with up to 68 percent sugar in them? If we do, then we must also expect our children to suffer from dental cavities, overweight, emotional problems, learning difficulties, hyperactivity, and worse. Of course, there will be some children and adults who seemingly escape the devastating results of junk food, but sooner or later even the healthiest person is going to be affected, and the next generation and the next will continue to pay a price. When we disturb our endocrine system, we ruin our body chemistry and endanger our health.

Although we are stressing the importance of our endocrine system in this chapter, this does not mean that other systems or organs of our body are not important. We briefly mentioned our liver and its important role in the regulation of our blood sugar. For example, one of the things that our liver does is to store some sugar and also to convert some sugar into glycogen (animal or liver-starch). This substance is stored in both our liver and muscle tissues. When we are in need of sugar, the liver will simply convert glycogen back into sugar. The same stress that affects our adrenal glands also affects such organs as the liver. For not only is the liver involved in the formation of blood and the metabolism of carbohydrates, protein, fats, minerals, and vitamins, the liver—among other things—also helps our blood to excrete waste materials, poisons, unneeded hormones, and bacteria.

Our liver is busy enough without the additional stress we

add to it in the form of alcohol, caffeine, nicotine, trauma, toxic drugs, poisons from our environment, and so on. Upon reflection, it becomes clear that some of the junk foods we eat and drink affect our body in several ways. By negatively affecting the glandular, gastrointestinal, vascular, and nervous systems, we are making sure that our body is sufficiently mixed up to disturb our mind. For example, alcohol is bad for our liver, our endocrine system, and our brain.

In the case of hypoglycemia, we can quickly see how alcohol will stimulate our adrenal glands to release adrenalin, which stimulates the liver to release sugar, which stimulates the pancreas to release insulin, which will depress our blood sugar levels, which leads to a need for more alcohol. This cycle will be repeated again and again. Addiction and ill health will follow. The same holds true for caffeine and nicotine. These drugs affect our adrenal glands, liver, and pancreas, and in addition stimulate our nervous system (alcohol will depress the nervous system).

Since our brain is an electrochemical computer, it does not require the mind of a Sherlock Holmes to see that alcohol, caffeine, nicotine, and sugar will negatively affect both our body and mind. Our electrochemical computer needs sugar to function. It requires a steady and sufficient amount of blood sugar to be delivered to it at all times. The brain and our entire nervous system needs the right amounts of sugar for proper functioning, but cannot get this from the refined sugar that we dump directly into our bloodstream, as we have already discussed. When there is a shortage of blood sugar (usually the direct result of the use of junk food and other harmful substances), then our brain which regulates such autonomic (independent, spontaneous) functions as our heartbeat, digestion, and breathing cannot do its job. That's why hypoglycemics suffer from symptoms like dizziness, palpitations, headaches, shakes, etc. It's the result of malfunctioning of the central nervous system, combined with an outpouring of excess adrenalin and other actions by the endocrine system.

Just as the chemical factories in our bodies are interrelated and interdependent, so it is with the various parts of the central nervous system. For example, the hypothalamus regulates our body temperature, certain metabolic processes, and autonomic activities; however, it is also regarded as the seat of our emotions. The hypothalamus, as the central point of our emotional behavior, is tied in with inputs from the cerebral cortex (cognitive-perceptual inputs), as well as inputs from our endocrine system. It is thought that the ventromedial (front and middle) portion of the hypothalamus acts as a stimulating mechanism, and that the lateral (back) portion of the hypothalamus acts as an inhibitory mechanism for our appetites. Again, it is believed that this so-called "appestat" is regulated by blood sugar levels.

When we begin to understand the influence of low blood sugar on both our body and mind, it becomes a little easier to accept the neurotic disturbances we so frequently find in people who suffer from hypoglycemia. Unfortunately, most of the people who demonstrate neurotic behavior are not even considered to perhaps suffer from low blood sugar. These people frequently receive the exact opposite treatment they need. For example, they may be treated with Valium and other drugs, which only make the condition worse; and they may even wind up in mental hospitals.

A rather celebrated case of such mistreatment was described in the *Detroit Free Press,* during the summer of 1980. This article explained how Stan Papi, of the Detroit Tigers, had been brought back from the "brink." According to this newspaper account, Stan Papi started to have some symptoms in 1974, while still a rookie for the St. Louis Cardinals. His shakes and palpitations scared him, and his doctor gave him Valium, on which he got worse and worse. Via Valium addiction he wound up with a psychiatrist who helped Papi to "blame his father and his wife" and placed him on some other drugs. Ultimately, in 1975, Papi went "berserk" and found himself in a mental hospital. There he received shock treatments, all to no avail. But, by the grace of God, an old lady across the street from his parents told them about her bout with hypoglycemia. When Papi's parents took their son out of the hospital and to a doctor who administered the GTT, it was only elementary to secure a cure, for Papi indeed suffered from hypoglycemia. In eight weeks' time Papi was on the road to good health and a career with the Tigers.

Now this is a celebrated case only because of Papi's stature as a member of the Tigers and his courage to reveal the story to the press. However, there is nothing remarkable about the story itself, for we see it all the time. Alcoholic after alcoholic, hyperactive child after hyperactive child, obese person after obese person, and depressed person after depressed person undergoes a transformation once it has been established that hypoglycemia is at the root of the problem. The plain truth is that emotional problems very often have a physical basis, and it is irresponsible to treat anyone for emotional problems without a *thorough* inquiry into his or her physical health.

While physical stimuli by themselves may not set the direction of our emotional responses, there is no doubt about their influence on our emotions. We need to think in terms of somatopsychogenic and psychosomatogenic relationships, and approach problems from this holistic point of view. Why organic conditions dispose some of us toward anger, others to depression, and again others to other negative emotions is undoubtedly related to the way we think. We simply cannot separate our thinking from the evaluation of perceptual-cognitive and/or proprioceptive stimuli.

HYPOCLYCEMIA II
SUBJECTIVE FINDINGS

A major difficulty in the treatment of hypoglycemia has been the fact that its symptoms may very well be those of many other physical and/or mental conditions. However, this problem is not as big as we are often told. When we have subjective histories of hypoglycemia, and no other definitive diagnosis (with consequently successful treatment!) has been made, then—regardless even of the outcome of objective hypoglycemia test findings—there is nothing to lose and everything to gain by trying out the antihypoglycemia diet. This is a healthy diet which is far better than the diets commonly followed by most of us.

On the other hand, the subjective indications of hypoglycemia are as a rule also established by objective test results—e.g., with the six-hour Glucose Tolerance Test (GTT).

The following is a questionnaire we can administer to ourselves and see how many of the possible hypoglycemia symptoms are applicable to us. We assign a value of 1 point to those questions that we answer with "sometimes," and 2 points to those questions we answer with "often." When we have a total score of 20 points, there is at least an indication that we may have hypoglycemia. However, it is not a good practice to make too many hard and fast rules. We may have only one symptom frequently and still have hypoglycemia, or we may have several symptoms and still not have hypoglycemia. The best way to find out is to have a holistically oriented physician evaluate our medical history, including the subjective and objective indicators of possible hypoglycemia, before establishing a treatment program that is exclusively tailored to our particular needs.

HYPOGLYCEMIA QUESTIONNAIRE

	OFTEN	SOMETIMES
1. Allergies		
2. Angry		
3. Antisocial behavior		
4. Anxious*		
5. Arthritis		
6. Asocial behavior		
7. Asthma		
8. Eczema		
9. Blackouts		
10. Bleeding gums		
11. Blurred vision		
12. Changes in moral conduct		
13. Clammy skin		
14. Cold extremities		
15. Cold sweats*		
16. Compulsive behavior		
17. Convulsions		
18. Crying without specific reason		
19. Depression*		
20. Digestive problems		
21. Disturbing dreams		
22. Dizziness*		

23. Drowsiness*   _____   _____
24. Dry mouth   _____   _____
25. Edema   _____   _____
26. Easily angry over
    small annoyances*   _____   _____
27. Easily out of breath   _____   _____
28. Easily tired   _____   _____
29. Excessive sweating   _____   _____
30. Exhaustion*   _____   _____
31. Fearfulness   _____   _____
32. Feel fatigued   _____   _____
33. Feel faint*   _____   _____
34. Feel better after breakfast   _____   _____
35. Feel shaky or have
    sudden shakes   _____   _____
36. Feel worse after breakfast   _____   _____
37. Great desire (need) for
    alcohol*   _____   _____
38. Great desire (need) for
    caffeine*   _____   _____
39. Great desire (need) to eat
    often   _____   _____
40. Great desire (need) for
    nicotine*   _____   _____
41. Great desire (need) for
    sweets   _____   _____
42. Hand tremors   _____   _____
43. Hay fever   _____   _____
44. Headaches*   _____   _____
45. Heart palpitations*   _____   _____
46. Heart flutterings   _____   _____
47. Hives   _____   _____
48. Hungry between meals
    (suddenly)*   _____   _____
49. Inability to concentrate*   _____   _____
50. Inability to go back to sleep*   _____   _____
51. Inability to go to sleep*   _____   _____
52. Inability to make decisions*   _____   _____
53. Inability to handle pressures   _____   _____
54. Inability to remember things*   _____   _____
55. Incoordination   _____   _____

56. Insecure _____ _____
57. Irritable (especially before eating)* _____ _____
58. Itching skin _____ _____
59. Lack of coordination _____ _____
60. Lack of energy (stamina/zest) _____ _____
61. Lack of initiative _____ _____
62. Lack of self-control _____ _____
63. Lack of sexual desire _____ _____
64. Leg cramps _____ _____
65. Midafternoon headaches _____ _____
66. Midmorning headaches* _____ _____
67. Midafternoon need for sweets _____ _____
68. Midmorning need for sweets* _____ _____
69. Mood swings _____ _____
70. Muscle pains* _____ _____
71. Must eat whenever nervous _____ _____
72. Must have coffee or cigarette first thing in A.M. _____ _____
73. Numbness* _____ _____
74. Neurodermatitis _____ _____
75. Nervous breakdowns _____ _____
76. Nervousness* _____ _____
77. Overactive _____ _____
78. Overweight/obese* _____ _____
79. Phobias _____ _____
80. Rapid pulse* _____ _____
81. Seizures _____ _____
82. Sleepy after meals _____ _____
83. Reduction of sex drive _____ _____
84. Rhinitis _____ _____
85. Sensitive to slight noises _____ _____
86. Sighing _____ _____
87. Sinusitis _____ _____
88. Stomach cramps (or uneasiness) _____ _____
89. Suicidal tendencies _____ _____
90. Temper tantrums _____ _____
91. Tremors* _____ _____
92. Ticks or muscle spasms _____ _____

93. Twitching of eyelids   _____   _____
94. Unconsciousness   _____   _____
95. Unsociable behavior   _____   _____
96. Vertigo*   _____   _____
97. Very emotional   _____   _____
98. Very tired   _____   _____
99. Very worried*   _____   _____
100. Yawning   _____   _____

The more common symptoms of hypoglycemia have been marked with an asterisk (*). These symptoms, however, like any of the other symptoms listed in the questionnaire, only indicate the possibility of this widespread disorder. The next thing you need is a six-hour Glucose Tolerance Test (GTT). If you scored twenty or more points on the subjective test, and especially if several of the asterisked symptoms are included, then the chances are very high that you will have an abnormal GTT. Yet, even when the findings of the GTT are within normal levels, and you suffer from subjective symptoms, you are still advised to try the antihypoglycemia diet. When refined carbohydrates make us feel bad, and the absence thereof makes us feel better, we would be very foolish indeed to fail to listen. Also, there are many other ways, in addition to the GTT, in which we can investigate the presence of hypoglycemia and its varied causes—e.g., adrenal, pituitary, and/or pancreatic dysfunction, alcoholism, drug addiction, obesity, liver disease, schizophrenia, etc. (Tintera 1949, 1951, 1955, 1966, 1967). However, the most common cause for hypoglycemia is found in our self-defeating life-styles, which may lead to such conditions as hypoadrenocorticism (Light, *Homeostasis Revisited,* 1981; *Hypoglycemia,* 1982; Tintera, 1955).

HYPOGLYCEMIA III
OBJECTIVE FINDINGS

The most popular and most widely accepted medical test for hypoglycemia is the so-called Glucose Tolerance Test (GTT). This test requires that we drink 100 grams of glucose (50 grams in Britain), after having a carbohydrate rich diet for at least three days and fasting for the preceding twelve hours. This test shows such things as our fasting blood sugar level, and the blood sugar levels at various intervals after we drink the glucose. However, some of the more important things that the test reveals is the speed whereby our blood sugar level falls and the level to which it falls.

According to medical manuals in use in this country, our blood sugar level should not fall below 70 mg. per 100 cc. of blood. However, experts in the field of hypoglycemia insist that the normal range is from 80-120 mg. per 100 cc. of blood. The ideal blood sugar level is seen by some as 100 mg. per 100 cc. of blood (Page, *Your Body Is Your Best Doctor,* 1972).

However, even the experts have some disagreements as to what constitutes normal and abnormal readings. That is why the subjective and objective findings need to be used together. There is really no such thing as a GTT that is a little bit low, for the obvious truth is that what is a *little* low on a standardized objective test may well be *very* low for that particular person. Usually we do not have a well established base line that tells us what that particular person's normal blood sugar levels are. We have different normal metabolic rates, pulse rates, and body temperatures, and we also have different blood chemistry.

Tests can provide us with guidance; however, they cannot provide all the answers in making a correct diagnosis. The experts do agree, however, that the speed at which blood sugar levels rise or fall is very important in helping to make a correct diagnosis. Glucose tolerance curves may vary widely, and so-called "abnormal" curves may be due to a number of abnormalities including acromegaly, Addison's disease, alcoholism, alimentary glycosuria, anorexia nervosa, brain injury, Cushing's pituitary basophilism, diabetes mellitus, drug abuse, emotional stress, hemochromatosis, hyperinsulinism, hyperthyroidism, hypoadrenocorticism, hypogonadism, insulin shock, myasthenia gravis, myxedema, pituitary deficiency, pituitary fatigue, reactive hypoglycemia, renal glycosuria, Simmond's disease, etc. Blood glucose disturbances are also frequently found concomitant with manic-depression, schizophrenia, various toxic states, viral disease, the use of birth control pills, tranquilizers, etc.

Solid interpretation of *abnormal* glucose tolerance curves

usually requires the assistance of trained health professionals. A thorough evaluation for hypoglycemia must also include a complete physical examination, personal and family medical history, nutritional evaluation, and additional tests such as a complete blood count, urinalysis, thyroid profile (PBI, T_3, T_4), and urinary 17-Ketosteroids. The oral glucose tolerance test, as part of a thorough health evaluation, is an excellent aid in the proper diagnosis and treatment of both physical and psychological disorders. It is unfortunate, however, that glucose tolerance curves are all too frequently considered normal, while standard medical textbooks (e.g., Flint and Cain, 1975), and rewpected medical laboratory textbooks (e.g., Bauer, 1982) and hypoglycemia specialists (e.g. Abrahamson, *Behavior Approaches to Weight Control*, 1977; Airola, *Hypoglycemia: A Better Approach*, 1977; Cleave, *The Saccharine Disease*, 1975; Fredericks, *Low Blood Sugar and You*, 1969; Tintera, 1955) maintain that they are not!

In *Emergency Treatment and Management* (Flint and CAin, 1975) which can be found in virtually every physician's office and in every hospital in this country, the *normal* blood glucose values are listed as 80-120 mg./dl. This is also precisely what the experts maintain is the normal range. Unfortunately, we find that laboratories and physicians throughout the country are applying widely varying standards ranging from 56-104 to 85-125 mg./dl. Experience, however, has shown that for a healthy mind and body it it important to have a relatively steady level of glucose which is not to fall below 80 nor to rise above 120 mg./dl. Blood sugar levels below 70 mg./dl. often lead to subclinical medical and psychological problems, and blood sugar levels below 50 mg./dl. will lead to serious clinical problems.

The oral Glucose Tolerance Test (GTT) is normal when the fasting blood sugar is 80-120 mg./dl. One hour following the drinking of the glucose, the blood sugar level should rise about 50 percent (but ideally to less than 160 mg./dl.). Two hours following the drinking of the glucose, the blood sugar level should return to the fasting level and remain there for the duration of the test. I agree with Marilyn Hamilton Light *(Ho-*

meostasis Revisited, 1981) that "any variation should be considered abnormal." However, please remember, as I said earlier, that tests cannot provide us with all the answers in making a correct diagnosis.

Below is a diagram of the normal range of blood sugar levels. We can superimpose the findings of our own GTT on this if necessary.

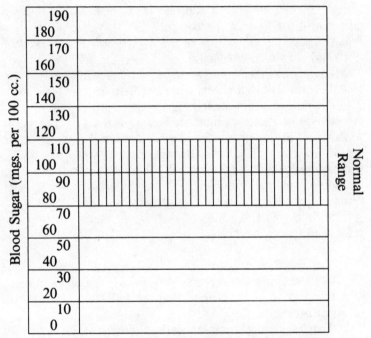

1 Hr. 2 Hr. 3 Hr. 4 Hr. 5 Hr. 6 Hr.
Time-lapse after ingesting glucose.

HYPOGLYCEMIA IV
DO'S AND DON'TS

As we have previously explained, the GTT by itself is of little value. We need a competent physician to evaluate all the findings, including those of a thorough physical examination, careful history, as well as the GTT and possibly other tests. After all this has been done and it has been decided that corrective action for hypoglycemia is indicated, then we need to remind ourselves that this is one of the stress disorders. Thus, in the treatment of hypoglycemia we need more than dietary change. In fact, we need a change in our life-style. The answer to the problem will be found in a holistic approach, which includes (1) *better nutrition,* (2) *vitamin and mineral supplements* (because of past malnutrition we quite likely have certain nutritional deficiencies, and in addition it has been found that specific supplements may be helpful), (3) *exercise,* (4) *rest and relaxation,* (5) *hobbies,* (6) *a program of emotional reeducation,* and (7) *spiritual renewal.*

Many people have asked for specific dietary information and wish for clear-cut diet sheets which explain exactly what to do. There is no exact diet for hypoglycemics. All that can be given are general guidelines which are based on the fact that we are so different in our physical and emotional makeup. For example, it has been found that orange juice is well tolerated by some hypoglycemics, but not with others; that potatoes are bad for some, yet are quite all right for others. However, some things seem to apply to all hypoglycemics.

The following are some of the things that hypoglycemics may need to do:

1. Eat about six small meals a day. No meal should leave us "stuffed." Individual differences will quickly tell us the number of meals and amounts of food that are indicated for our optimum health.

2. Eat high-fiber, natural carbohydrates, such as whole grains, seeds, nuts, vegetables, and fruits.

3. Eat only *hot* cereals for breakfast, such as buckwheat, millet, oats, etc. Hot cereals digest slowly.

4. In-between snacks may consist of seeds, nuts, fruit, juice, yogurt, or milk. (However, it is to be noted that too much milk is not good for our general health, especially nowadays, because of Strontium 90, DDT, and residues of antibiotics. See Page, *Your Body Is Your Best Doctor,* 1972.)

5. Get some protein every day. Do not overuse protein as is sometimes recommended.

6. Find out what supplemental vitamins and minerals may be needed. Many hypoglycemics need to take extra C, E, and B-complex, brewers yeast, and other supplements (Airola, *Hypoglycemia: A Better Approach,* 1977).

7. Use fruit in preference over juices. Dilute juices with water, as needed.

The following are some of the things that hypoglycemics definitely must *not* do:

1. Eat any refined sugar (glucose, dextrose, etc.) and any product that contains sugar in any amount.

2. Eat any white flour, or any product made with white flour, such as pizzas, pies, cakes, etc.

3. Use refined starch products such as macaroni, noodles, spaghetti, etc.

4. Use alcohol.

5. Use nicotine.

6. Use caffeine (coffee, tea, cocoa, chocolate).

7. Use soft drinks that contain sugar or artificial sweeteners.

8. Buy nonprescription drugs (such as APC's, aspirin, Bromo-Seltzer) that contain caffeine. Also be careful with prescription drugs; many of those also contain caffeine in large doses.

9. Use too much salt. The use of salt may lead to a drop in blood potassium (and blood sugar) and do damage to your health in general—e.g., through water retention, etc.

HYPOGLYCEMIA V
SOME NOT SO SUGARY FACTS

In the preceding pages we have looked closely at the most prevalent stress disorder in our society. If we are not yet convinced about the main culprit in this entire matter, we may want to have a few more reminders:

1. Sugar ($C_{12}H_{22}O_{11}$) is a dangerous substance which destroys our health and happiness. It is obtained in crystalline form, from cane and beets. Actually, it is a double sugar (disaccharide) composed of glucose and fructose.

2. Sugar is totally unnecessary for out diet.

3. Sugar disturbs our metabolism and removes essential B vitamins and minerals from our diet. This makes sugar a thief!

4. Sugar (sucrose, dextrose, glucose) is the purest edible substance we have. Purity does not mean that it is good for us. Cocaine and other dangerous substances can also be bought in pure state. In this case, pure means that the sugar has been refined so many times that every single valuable nutritious element has been removed. Consequently, sugar has absolutely zero nutritional value.

5. Sugar, while not providing any nutrition, does provide calories. These calories can and do turn into fat.

6. Sugar is primarily consumed in hidden form in the processed foods that we buy.

7. Sugar consumption in the USA has increased by over 1000 percent since 1821. It has been noted that our degenerative diseases, metabolic disorders, and such things as anitsocial behavior have also dramatically increased. Many experts suspect a direct relationship between the rise in ill health and the use of sugar.

8. The elimination of all sugar from our diet is the surest and healthiest way to reduce excess weight.

9. Americans consume an average of one hundred pounds of sugar every year, and another thirty-five pounds of corn sweeteners!

10. Sugar has been linked by researchers to diabetes, heart disease, hypoglycemia, and many other disorders.

11. Sucrose, glucose, and dextrose are essentially the same. Their molecular difference does not make any difference to our endocrine system, which is not able to deal directly with these substances. Bypassing our internal chemical factories leads to disaster.

12. Natural sugars are lactose (milk sugar), maltose (malt sugar), and fructose (fruit sugar). Hypoglycemics need to be careful even in the use of these products.

13. For our bodies to function correctly, we need a certain balance of glucose in our blood with a certain amount of oxygen. This is accomplished by the adrenal glands. Any excessive stress (physical, environmental, emotional) may damage our adrenal glands. The easiest damage is done by the intake of refined sugar products.

14. Blackstrap molasses still contains 35 percent sucrose.

15. The people in the United States get an average of 24 percent empty calories in their diets (sugar), of which 18 percent is sucrose that has been added to processed foods. One quarter of our total food intake consists of empty calories that disturb our metabolism and destroy our health.

16. Eating sugar does *not* provide us with more sugar in our bloodstream. The quick rise in blood sugar is quickly depressed by insulin, and we end up with lower and lower blood sugar levels.

17. Our brain and nervous system burn only sugar. When our brain and nervous system do not get enough fuel, our physical and emotional health is directly in peril. The area of our brain that is most affected by sugar shortages is our emotional area; namely the limbic system, and in particular our hypothalamus. This is the system that controls our heartbeat, stomach contractions, intestinal activity, etc. Since very little sugar can be stored in our brain and nervous system, it is easy to understand that low blood sugar quickly leads to many of the symptoms we have described in the previous pages.

In summary, our body plays a very vital part in both our physical and emotional health. There is overwhelming evidence that our minds directly affect the well-being of our bodies, and that our bodies directly influence the well-being of our minds. As Christians, we are charged with the responsibility to take good care of our bodies. We are created in God's image, and our bodies are the dwelling-place for the Holy Spirit. God wants us to be as healthy and happy as we can possibly be, and holds us accountable for whatever he has given us. Any abuse of our bodies, and any willful neglect, by the consumption of dangerous products or through the display of a noncaring attitude ("I don't care; we all have to go sometime anyway"), cannot be pleasing to the Lord. In addition to the responsibility we have towards ourselves, we also have a social responsibility. Others look to us for guidance, and in particular our children do this.

Know ye not that ye are the temple of God, and that the Spirit of God dwelleth in you? If any man defile the temple of God, him shall God destroy; for the temple of God is holy, which temple ye are. (1 Corinthians 3:16, 17)

11 Do's and Don'ts for Good Physical Health

In the previous chapter we learned that in addition to paying close attention to our mental and spiritual lives, we also need to pay close attention to our physical lives. Undoubtedly we have also come to the conclusion that the holistic approach is best for our health and happiness. We cannot afford to overlook the interdependence and interrelationship of our body, mind, and soul. If we are interested in staying alive as long and happily as possible, then we need to pay attention to some of the research findings and observations that tell us how to increase our health and longevity.

Unfortunately, there is a certain amount of confusion even among Christians, who view quick suicide as something that is inherently wrong, yet somehow fail to see the type of suicide that is done slowly. As long as we continue to do harmful things to ourselves, we are adding to the already existing genetic and environmental problems. Overeating, overworking, overdoing anything is not good for us. Ingesting dangerous products, from marijuana to cocaine, from caffeine to nicotine, and from sugar-pop to alcohol, *is* destructive. Many of us are quite concerned about people who "drink"; yet we are often doing equally destructive things to our own bodies with the products that we consume. For example, it has been reported that the moderate use of alcohol (although never good for us) is not as bad for our health as the use of caffeine.

Much of our confusion is the result of social pressures, social customs, and the fact that many destructive and dangerous products are declared legal and natural by unscrupulous manufacturers and advertisers. Because something is legal does not necessarily mean that it is good for us. Just because something is natural does not mean that it will not kill us. The confusion is perhaps nowhere more apparent than in the way we treat our children. Most people refuse to give them coffee, yet think nothing of giving them cola drinks, cocoa, or chocolate. Yet, all these products have high caffeine contents.

The Lord has told us to seek "wisdom and understanding," and this is precisely what we need to do. For certainly with wisdom and understanding we would not go on harming ourselves. In the meantime, millions and millions of us are definitely addicted to a number of dangerous substances, ranging from food to drink, and from illegal chemicals to fumes. Just as there is no difference between the woman who is a little bit pregnant and the one who is a lot pregnant, there is no difference between the person who is addicted to alcohol, nicotine, caffeine, or sugar. An addiction is an addiction! So long as we *have to have* certain things that are proven destructive to our health, we are not free.

Many people in official capacities will not tell us the truth about our destructive behavior. They will not teach us better ways, for they assume that we are not interested in hearing the truth. Most of the time, we are getting a mixture of what we like to hear, and what people in authority and power believe will keep them there. The surest way to become rich and powerful is to deliver to the people what they want, whether or not it kills them. The surest way to become unpopular is to tell the truth, especially if it goes contrary to carnal desires. However, as Christians we do not want to be dishonest. In Colossians 3:9 we read, "Lie not one to another."

When we open our eyes to the truth and observe the life of Jesus, we certainly will conclude that he never did anything that was destructive to others or to himself. We must not mingle the truth with half-truth, carnal things with spiritual things, and we must not participate in the deceptions of this world. In the carnal world we are told what we like to hear, but in the spiritual world we hear the things that are good for us. Many books are written not to tell us the truth, but to tell us what we want to hear. As Christians we need to look for the things that are good for us, even if we do not like them. In this chapter we will discuss some do's and don'ts in the belief that these suggestions will help us lead healthier and happier lives. The information is based on data that has consistently been reported by researchers and experts in various fields and is based on many findings, even by the United States government.

HERE ARE THE DON'TS

Do not smoke.
Smoking is considered one of the most dangerous and destructive habits found in human beings. In the United States, cigarette smoking contributes to 300,000 deaths every year, not to mention ill health for many hundreds of thousands more. It is said that each and every cigarette smoked by heavy smokers reduces their life span by about six minutes. The short-term effects of smoking include an increase in our pulse rate, a rise in our blood pressure, and a reduction in our skin temperature. Our heartbeat may increase up to 40 percent, and parts of our central nervous system may be stimulated and then depressed (reduced). A decrease in appetite and physical endurance is commonly found. Smoking also affects our blood sugar levels, through the effect of the nicotine on the adrenal glands. These glands will produce excessive amounts of hormones which lead the liver to release sugar, which in turn leads to a drop in blood sugar levels due to action taken by our pancreas. Blood sugar levels may rise as high as 36 percent as the result of cigarette smoking (Adams & Murray, *Is Low Blood Sugar Making You a Nutritional Cripple?*, 1975).

The long-term effects are even more serious, leading to many ailments including peripheral vascular disease (narrowing or blockage of blood vessels in our extremities), chronic respiratory problems, bronchitis, emphysema (loss of lung elasticity leading to retention of too much air), lung, stomach, intestinal, throat and other cancers. Women who smoke have a tendency to give premature birth and also have smaller babies.

Smoking seriously reduces our physical fitness, impairs our overall health, affects our endocrine and central nervous systems, and may contribute to emotional problems. Smoking is also destructive to the lives of those around us. Many physicians have quit smoking; however, many others continue to be addicted.

It has also been reported that in the United States we annually spend seven billion dollars for health care as the direct result of smoking. The tobacco industry and many special interest groups earn a lot of money from the horrible suffering of our nicotine addicts. Future historians may refuse to believe that "enlightened" governments allowed the unhindered growth of tobacco crops. Tobacco use, according to Joseph A. Califano, Jr. (1981), our former secretary of HEW, "has killed more Americans, more painfully than all our wars and all our traffic accidents combined."

It is *not* true that it is very difficult to quit smoking. It *is* true that it is impossible to quit smoking, unless we want to! When the hypoglycemia diet and other health instructions listed in this book are followed, it will make quitting a lot easier. The reason why so many people undergo physical discomfort when they quit is due to a number of factors, including *nicotine tolerance* (our system has made adjustments and now misses the nicotine), *low blood sugar levels,* and *psychological dependence.* Headaches, dizziness, irritability, restlessness, and even depression may appear as withdrawal symptoms. These are not bad signs. Interpret them as the beginning of a better, freer, healthier life. It may be ten to fourteen days before all of the symptoms disappear. When we quit smoking, it is very important to follow a healthy, natural diet, free of refined carbohydrates (in particular sugar), get plenty of fresh air and exercise, and ensure that we use a good multiple vitamin and mineral supplement. In particular, extra vitamin C is needed to help in the detoxification of our bodies.

Do not use alcohol.

Alcohol is a dangerous drug, involved in untold misery, numerous crimes (including manslaughter), and the destruction of our overall health and happiness. The short-term effect of alcohol is that it acts as a depressant on our central nervous system, disturbs our blood sugar levels, and provides us with empty calories. Long-term effects include damage to our liver, heart, and other body organs. Both short- and long-term effects include accidents, serious poisoning, and suicides. Alcohol abuse leads to a general deterioration of our health, seriously affects our nervous and endocrine systems, and leads to such manifestations as tremors, agitation, hallucinations, etc.

Continued use of alcohol leads to both physical and psychological dependence. The combination of alcohol with antihistamines, barbiturates, tranquilizers, and many other drugs is extremely dangerous. It has never been established that even the use of small quantities of alcohol is safe. Virtually all alcoholics have been found to be hypoglycemic (Airola, *Hypoglycemia: A Better Approach,* 1977). Not much change in the rise of alcoholism may be expected unless there is an absolute turning away from refined carbohydrates and a growth of good educational programs and dietary practices early in the lives of our children.

It is well established that alcoholic beverages have virtually no food value, are high in calories, and that they poison our body, in particular our liver and brain. The use of alcoholic beverages makes it very difficult to maintain and/or attain correct weight. Alcohol is indirectly responsible for untold destruction and carnage on our highways, the destruction of families, and the loss of jobs, homes, and fortunes.

Do not eat refined carbohydrates.

Since carbohydrates are our most immediate source of energy, we may find it difficult to understand that we must be careful with them. While our caloric intake may consist of roughly 50 percent carbohydrates, it is *essential* that they are of the unrefined kind. Consequently, sugar and white flour are definitely out, and the carbohydrates that we obtain from vegetables, fruits, and whole grains are definitely in. When we refrain from the use of refined carbohydrates, we will get an increase in our steady energy levels. High-fiber, natural carbohydrates are slowly converted into sugar and as the sugar enters our bloodstream slowly, this leads to the prevention of excessive insulin production. Refined carbohydrates, on the other hand, quickly enter our bloodstream and are also quickly lost, especially when our pancreas produces too much insulin.

Actually, it is important that we discover how much carbohydrate our particular bodies and life-style require. While 50 percent has been set as an average, this may not be enough for some of us, and too much for others. Excessive consumption of refined carbohydrates will definitely lead to malnutrition. The more junk foods we eat, the unhealthier we get.

The excessive use of carbohydrates depletes the vitamin B in our bodies; yet this same vitamin is needed to burn off excessive carbohydrates. Carbohydrates are needed to break down protein into energy and to help with the efficient utilization of fats. More about the importance of unrefined carbohydrates may be learned in Chapter 10.

Do not use caffeine.
In the previous chapter we have already described what caffeine does to people who suffer from hypoglycemia; however, it needs to be recognized that caffeine is truly a harmful drug for all of us. It is harmful because of its negative effects on our central nervous system, leading to "caffeinism," manifested in anxiety, restlessness, excitement, insomnia, nervousness, irregular heartbeats, and many other symptoms. Caffeine is also deleterious for our endocrine system, leading to blood sugar disturbances, manifested in all the previously mentioned symptoms and many others (see Chapter 10).

Caffeine is found not only in coffee (100 mg. of caffeine per cup), but also in many other popular products such as tea (60-75 mg. caffeine per cup), cola drinks (40-60 mg. caffeine per glass), cocoa (50-250 mg. per cup), chocolate, and many other products including prescription drugs such as Darvon, Fiorinal, and others. In addition, caffeine is added to many over-the-counter drugs such as Anacin, aspirin, Bromo-Seltzer, and others. Virtually all of the so-called weight-control medicines contain from 100-600 mg. of caffeine per daily dosage. The cumulative caffeine intake of unsuspecting consumers is really staggering. The most commonly used caffeine product is coffee. This product has also been linked with many other physical ailments, including an increase in fatty substances in the blood, irregular heart rhythms, and cancer, particularly of the pancreas. The cancer is *not* thought to be due to caffeine but some other substance found in coffee.

It has frequently been pointed out that the use of caffeine in combination with sugar is truly disastrous. The caffeine starts the sugar cycle going by its effect on the adrenal glands, and the sugar has a direct effect on the pancreas. Cola drinks are especially bad for our health because of the combined caffeine-sugar attack on our endocrine system, *and* high acidity levels. Many experts agree on the dangers of caffeine. Disagreement comes primarily from the industry involved in caffeine products, and unfortunately many of the addicts themselves.

HERE ARE THE DO'S

Do maintain your correct weight.
One of the more important things for good physical health is to maintain our correct weight. Of course, we all know that it is difficult to know exactly what our correct weight should be. Many of us erroneously believe that the so-called "ideal weight" from life insurance company weight charts indicate our correct weight. However, it seems more logical that our correct weight is the weight that is good for our physical, mental, and spiritual health.

The Scriptures are abundantly clear that God wants us healthy and happy and to refrain from excesses of all kinds. He wants us to be reasonable in all things. In Proverbs 23:20, 21 we read, "Be not among winebibbers; among riotous eaters of flesh: for the drunkard and the glutton shall come to poverty: and drowsiness shall clothe a man with rags." And again in Proverbs 30:8 we find, ". . . give me neither poverty nor riches; feed me with food convenient for me. . . ." Indeed, there are scores of Scriptures which show that God wants us to be careful with our bodies as well as our minds. In Psalm 141:3, 4 we read, "Set a watch, O Lord, before my mouth; keep the door of my lips."

At those times when we feel weak and believe that we have no choice but to overeat, then we need to look once again at God's Word. In 1 Corinthians 10:13 we are reminded, "God is faithful, who will not suffer you to be tempted above that ye are able; but will with the temptation also make a way to escape, that ye may be able to bear it." A way of escape from temptation is to utilize our minds as objectively as possible, to learn more about our emotions, and to guide our thinking, feelings, and actions.

Of course, we need to be very careful that we do not judge anyone in these matters. All of us are fallible; none of us is righteous; all of us have sinned; all of us come short of the glory of God. It is only through the blood of Jesus that we have hope for today and for tomorrow. How excellent is the warning in Romans 14:23, "And he that doubteth is damned if he eat, because he eateth not of faith: for whatsoever is not of faith is sin." Undoubtedly, we need to be mindful that "Whether therefore ye eat, or drink, or whatsoever ye do, do all to the glory of God" (1 Corinthians 10:31).

To maintain our correct weight we need to establish what we believe is good for our health and happiness. The so-called ideal weight tables have come under heavy attack by many experts. It has been found that being over the ideal weight on these tables does not necessarily lead to a shortened life span; however, it has also been shown that *obesity* does lead to a shortened life span. Obesity is truly devastating to us, for it often leads to diabetes, high blood pressure, increased cholesterol levels, etc. While some of us who fit neatly into the ideal weight scales may well be more susceptible to illness and disease, those who grossly exceed the standard weights are endangered by even more serious illnesses and problems. The responsibility for weight control is obviously a very personal one.

Many explanations have been given why some of us are overweight and others are not. However, it is believed that virtually *all* of the overweight people in this country can lose a good deal of weight (Brandt, *A Guide to Rational Weight Control*, 1980) and that it is unwise to search for excuses rather than ways to solve the problem. Apparently, except for a *very* small percentage (less than 1 percent) we can learn to control our weight. Even when we have certain glandular disorders, there is much that can be done. The truth seems to be that in virtually all cases we have become overweight because we have eaten too much of the wrong kinds of food, and did not obtain sufficient amounts of exercise to burn up the excess calories. If the guidelines in this book are insufficient to help us learn to control our weight, we may wish to obtain a copy of *A Guide to Rational Weight Control.* Information as to where we can obtain this book is listed in the reference section. However, in most cases we find that as long as we follow the guidelines of this book our weight will get closer to that which is correct for us.

The reasons for this are very simple, for (1) the exclusion of refined carbohydrates, (2) the start of a regular exercise program, and (3) the elimination of dangerous substances such as caffeine, nicotine, and alcohol will all have *immediate* beneficial effects. However, if we want to learn the principles of weight control, we first need to learn the principles of reeducative self-counseling as described in this book. Then we need to learn some essentials about good nutrition, reduce our caloric intake, and increase our caloric output.

To get an idea if we are really burning up all those calories we consume, we may want to have a look at the table below, which has been prepared by the U.S. government (Home and Garden Bulletin #232), and which shows the energy expenditure by a 150-pound person in various activities:

ACTIVITY	CALORIES PER HOUR
Lying down or sleeping	80
Sitting	100
Driving an automobile	120
Standing	140
Domestic work	180
Walking, 2½ mph.	210
Bicycling, 5½ mph.	210

Gardening 220
Golf; lawn mowing with power mower 250
Bowling 270
Walking, 3¾ mph. 300
Swimming, ¼ mph. 300
Square dancing; volleyball; roller skating 350
Wood chopping or sawing 400
Tennis 420
Skiing, 10 mph. 600
Squash and handball 600
Bicycling, 13 mph. 660
Running, 10 mph. 900

As we can clearly see, there is a tremendous difference between sitting around, taking a walk (takes nearly three times as many calories as sitting around), driving a car, or riding a bike. The importance of exercise, however, goes beyond the burning of calories, and we will discuss this later. The more closely we follow a holistic point of view, paying close attention to our physical, mental, and spiritual health, the more closely shall we reach our desired weight goals. Eating disabilities rarely have only one cause, and thus we are well advised to look at all the areas of our lives.

Do get regular exercise
From our discussion on weight control, it has already become clear that exercise is very important to our health. However, some of us who are in the greatest need unfortunately do not participate in any kind of exercise at all. We often hear excuses about lack of time, being too overweight, etc.; however, this is very self-defeating. Of course, there are only twenty-four hours in each day; yet all that most of us need to do is to rearrange our priorities. To exercise requires only a little bit of time and only a little bit of work, but a lot of desire!

Most of us can help ourselves, with God's help, to increased physical, emotional, and spiritual health. Coach Floyd Eby, in his book *Champions Forever* (1978), makes the point that we are wasting our time trying to help those who refuse to help themselves. He says, "I am wasting my time and the Lord's time if I try to help people who will not lift a finger to help themselves to follow God's program for their lives." How true this is. All we can do is provide information and encouragement, give suggestions, be good examples by modeling constructive behavior, and teach. Beyond that, however, we can do very little. Certainly we cannot think, choose, feel, and act for others. God has given each of us personal responsibility to choose wisely (Romans 14:12).

In his excellent book *Jesus Wants You Well,* C. S. Lovett (1973) explains in great detail the importance of exercise and makes the simple statement that Christians must exercise their bodies daily. If we are interested in optimum health, we have indeed no choice but to exercise. Our bodies have been designed (created) to be used. If we do not utilize our bodies, we will prematurely age, lose resistance to a variety of diseases, be more prone to emotional difficulties, and have less energy.

In Genesis 3:19 God tells us that we shall eat our bread by the sweat of our brow. If we don't do this, then our bodies may not be as healthy as they could have been. Lack of physical work and/or exercise leads to a shortening of our life span. In fact, about one-third of all so-called diseases of civilization are believed to be the result of a lack of exercise.

How does all this fit in with our Christian convictions? How does not exercising fit in with our desires to stay alive as long and to be as healthy as possible? Lack of physical work and/or exercise is self-defeating.

Hans Mohl quotes five European professors on the subject of exercise. The first one, Professor Noecker, points out that improved circulation is the best method to fight certain diseases. The second one, Professor Hollman, states that after forty, *only* exercise can retard the aging process. The third one, Professor Reindell, declares that only with enough physical exercise will our bodies be able to fight off heart infarcts. The fourth one, Professor Halhuber, maintains that when we participate regularly in some sport, we will have a three times better chance to live through a heart attack. The fifth one, Professor Mellerowics, explains that exercise will keep our energy levels high and will help to restore them when stricken with various old-age problems.

Whatever research we look at, from whatever country, there is a unanimous message that regular exercise is beneficial for the reduction of stress in our lives. Exercise is good for our health. Does this mean that all of us must immediately head for the road and start jogging? Of course not! Obviously, we must not start on any exercise program without first obtaining sound medical advice.

The main objective of exercise is to improve our circulation, to make our heart and lungs more effective and efficient, and ultimately to receive benefits throughout our entire body. The heart especially needs exercise, for the heart is a muscle and the only way to have healthy muscles is through exercise. After we have received appropriate medical advice, we will most likely still have some choices as to the form of exercise that we like the best. All of us can have some form of exercise, regardless of where we are. We have seen how people in wheelchairs can and do participate in exercise programs, and most of us will be able to do the same.

One thing we always need to do is to begin slowly. It is important to do some form of warm-up exercises before our actual exercises, and likewise to have a short cooling-off period after our exercises. For example, prior to running we could do some aerobic exercises, and following running, we could do some walking. Speaking of walking, the latter has been heralded as one of the most beneficial, least dangerous, least expensive forms of exercise for the majority of us.

Dr. Fred. A. Stutman (*The Doctor's Walking Book,* 1980) calls walking the perfect exercise because our bodies are designed for this natural function. When we participate in a planned and regular walking exercise program, we may attain the excellent health benefits that are described by the five professors, quoted by Hans Mohl. In other words, with a program of regular walking exercise we can get *sustained energy,* rather than bursts of energy that result from some other forms of exercise. We could compare this to the use of protein foods for sustained energy, and refined carbohydrates for short bursts of energy, with often bad consequences.

Even a walking program requires careful planning and starting off with short periods of time, for short distances, and only gradually increasing both. Dr. Stutman, in *The Doctor's Walking Book,* recommends starting with a slow pace (2 mph.), followed by a moderate pace (3 mph.), and finally followed by a fast pace (4 mph.). To increase our pace takes both training and time. In fact, we would start off by walking only fifteen minutes during our first and second week, thirty minutes during our third and fourth week, and forty-five minutes during our fifth and sixth week. Eventually, however, we would walk sixty minutes every other day for a distance of two miles at a slow pace, three miles at a moderate pace, and four miles at a fast pace. Dr. Stutman points out that distance is not important, but the amount of time we spend is important.

The President's Council of Physical Fitness and Sports (1979) lists ten reasons why exercise is so important for all of us:

1. Strength and endurance developed through regular exercise enables us to perform daily tasks with relative ease. We use only a small part of our physical reserve in routine activities.

2. Skill and agility gained through practice provide for economy of movement.

3. Poise and grace are by-products of efficient movement. They help us to feel at ease in social situations and are factors in good appearance.

4. Good muscle tone and posture can protect us from certain back problems caused by sedentary living.

5. Controlling our weight is mostly a matter of balancing our food intake with our exercise (or activity) output. Inactivity is often as critical as overeating in creeping overweight.

6. To the degree that physical activity helps control our weight, it will also aid in preventing degenerative diseases. Diseases of the heart and blood vessels, diabetes, and arthritis strike the obese more often and more seriously than they strike those of desirable weight.

7. Mounting evidence indicates that exercise is one of the factors in maintaining the health of the heart and blood vessels. Active people have fewer heart attacks and a better recovery rate from such attacks than the inactive.

8. Enjoyable exercise can provide relief from tension and serves as a safe and natural tranquilizer.

9. Feeling physically fit helps us to build a desirable self-concept. We need to see ourselves at our optimum physically as well as in other ways.

10. Dynamic fitness can help to protect us against accidents and may be a lifesaving factor in emergencies. Reacting quickly and with physical decisiveness may enable us to avert a serious accident.

Do get at least seven to eight hours of sleep.
A number of reports have indicated that for good health and longevity we need to have at least seven to eight hours of sleep every night. Sleep has been used as a cure for a variety of physical and emotional problems, and clearly is essential just to keep us going. The Scriptures tell us that the Lord gives sleep to his loved ones (Psalm 127:2). It is one of the many benefits of trusting in the Lord and following his advice. He tells us that we can have fearless "sweet" sleep (Proverbs 3:24). God wants us to sleep in peace so that we may regenerate and refresh ourselves, have bodies and minds that function at optimum levels, and be able to fully participate in all the activities of our lives.

During sleep our muscles relax, our heart rate is reduced, our blood pressure goes down, and our body temperature drops. Our body gets a rest, and so do our minds. In fact, sleep is essential for good mental health. All of us know what happens when we do not get the amount of sleep we need, for there will be a variety of physical and emotional problems. While we need about eighteen hours of sleep every day during the first year of our lives, and only about six hours in old age, it has been universally found that most adults need eight hours of sleep.

Sleep deprivation leads to physical ailments and mental confusion, and if severe enough, to neurosis and even psychosis. When we sleep soundly, we will forget both internal and external stressors which in our waking state would have provided various negative physical and mental reactions. The beneficial effect of sleep is often demonstrated in so-called sleep cures (lasting up to three weeks of twenty hours of sleep a day) for those who are suffering from severe mental stress, illness, or injury. Sleep is a healing and restoring mechanism. We need to pay just as much attention to our sleep patterns as to our thinking and eating patterns.

Develop healthy eating habits.
We have already discussed the importance of avoiding refined carbohydrates in our diet and hopefully abstaining from commonly used but nevertheless dangerous drugs such as caffeine, nicotine, and alcohol. There are a few more things at which we may want to look. This does not mean that we can discuss all the do's and don'ts for healthful living in this book. What we hope to achieve is that we will get motivated enough to continue to do reading and research on our own. We need to develop a conviction that it is our responsibility to look after the things that God has given to us, and that very much includes our bodies and minds.

One of the things that have been found to be of great importance in optimum functioning is to have a healthy breakfast every morning. Breakfast means that we are "breaking our fast." We have been without food for periods of perhaps twelve hours, and it is necessary for the proper functioning of our bodies to "refuel." Having breakfast not only helps us to get the necessary energy for our daily tasks, but it also helps us to keep healthier and live longer. Having breakfast has proven to be important in the prevention of accidents, the regulation of our metabolism, and many other things. It is startling that so many people with weight control problems do not eat breakfast. It is the one meal that will do them more good than harm.

In this chapter we have discussed some do's and don'ts for good physical and mental health. These are only a few suggestions. There are many more suggestions that could be made, such as eating mostly raw, natural, and poison-free foods, or to be careful not to consume an excessive amount of animal protein and to be careful with the water we drink (there are many increasing problems with the safety of our water supply).

It must be recognized that this book cannot provide all the information we need for a more rational way of life. We need to study on our own and seriously look into the facts. However, we need to be extra careful with the "facts" supplied by the drug, cosmetics, and food industries and those agencies that make their living from these industries.

Whether or not we follow the suggestions that have been given in this book, there is increasing evidence that the health of our mind is directly related to the health of our body. In fact, there cannot be a healthy mind unless there is a healthy brain. Our brain is very much a body organ which depends on nutrition, stimulation, oxygen, etc.

As Christians we have a very grave responsibility to ourselves and to others to improve and safeguard our health, and to improve and safeguard our environment. We need to be watchful for everything that is harmful whether in food, drink, household chemicals, or cosmetics. We also need to learn that undereating is far healthier than overeating, and that exercise is just as essential as rest and relaxation, and above all that the peace and joy in Christ will be all the greater when we know that we have been good stewards over the things that God has entrusted to us.

For example, merely eating *anything* in the morning is not good enough. Many millions of breakfasts consumed throughout the country are so bad that they are dangerous. While it is unwise to miss breakfast, it is worse to eat a heavy sugar-loaded breakfast than no breakfast. What we do need is a healthy breakfast, without refined carbohydrates of any kind. Ideally we have some protein, some unrefined carbohydrates, some fat, some water, and some vitamins and minerals. In short, we need a little of all the essential nutrients to insure that our bodies and minds will function at their very best.

In addition to eating *healthy* foods, we need to make sure that we get a *variety* of foods. Eating a balanced meal is more than making sure that we get enough protein, carbohydrates, etc. It also means that we get a good selection of grain products, vegetables, milk products, poultry, fish, eggs, dry peas and beans, etc. We do *not* eat a variety of foods if we merely change from steak to hamburgers to hot dogs!

In order to avoid too much fat, saturated fat, and cholesterol, we may simply choose lean meat, fish, poultry, dry beans and peas as good sources for protein. Many experts are advising us to reduce our intake of butter, cream, hydrogenated margarines, shortenings, coconut oil, and the foods that are made from these products. Other things we can do is to broil, bake, or boil rather than to fry foods.

One thing that undoubtedly most of us know by now is to be extremely careful with salt (sodium chloride). The dangers of salt have been so well researched and publicized that hopefully all of us have greatly reduced the use of this dangerous product. As we know, salt causes not only high blood pressure (and all the consequences thereof), but it also damages our kidneys, retains water in the body, and reduces the potassium level in our blood stream, which in turn also helps to lower our blood sugar levels. It is little wonder that salt makes us both thirsty and hungry. Of course, this is one of the reasons why manufacturers prefer to use heavy doses of salt in and on our foods, so that we will use more and more of their products.

The suggestions that have been made in this chapter are based on research findings that tell us we can increase our longevity by making some major changes in the way we are living. Obviously, with the increase in longevity comes an increase in good health, energy, and also of greater peace of mind. The health of our minds is closely tied in with the health of our bodies. The wisdom of the ancient philosophers that a healthy mind needs a healthy body is still as true as ever.

PART FIVE:

THE RENEWED MIND

And be not conformed to this world: but be ye transformed by the renewing of your mind, that ye may prove what is that good, and acceptable, and perfect will of God. (Romans 12:2)

12 How to Obtain a Renewed Mind

In this book we have discussed the renewal of our natural minds through objective thinking, and the renewal of our spiritual minds through faith and obedience. We have learned to appreciate the importance of understanding our emotions, and of having some objective rules for sound decision-making. We have also hopefully become proficient in a simple, yet highly efficient and safe system by which we can quickly analyze much of our behavior. This objective approach to problem-solving and learning new behavior has proven a great blessing to countless people. The renewal of our natural minds via Reeducative Self-Counseling is based on objectification and visualization.

Many of the preceding chapters have already laid the foundation for this chapter, which deals with the renewal of our spiritual minds. Even as we discussed the various steps involved in learning new self-enhancing behaviors we have steadily looked to the Scriptures. For whether we deal with natural or supernatural behavior, it is very clear that God is the ultimate source of all wisdom, knowledge, and understanding. While the renewal of our natural minds can be accomplished by most of us most of the time, it is only possible to obtain a renewed (spiritual) mind as a gift of God. In this chapter, whenever we talk about the "renewed mind," we are talking about the "mind of Christ within us." The mind is a gift of God to all who are believers in and followers of Jesus Christ as the Son of God.

The only way to have a renewed mind is to come to Jesus, accept him, follow him, and let him live within us. While we need to make a decision to do these things, it is even more clear that the renewed mind is a matter of sanctification. This means that only God can fill our empty but willing vessels. The renewal of our spiritual minds is a matter of doing away with the "old man" and of putting on the "new man, which is renewed in knowledge after the image of him that created him . . ." (Colossians 3:10). The putting on of the new man requires a faithful commitment to embrace the love of God actively as well as passively, and to let this love shine in our lives and the lives of others, through goodness, forgiveness, and fellowship.

After we decide to follow the Lord, and prepare ourselves as God has directed us to do, then he will fill us with his Spirit and do the sanctification. Thus, the renewed mind is a precious gift from God. An excellent prescription for obtaining the renewed mind is found in Ephesians 4:23-32:

> . . . and be renewed in the spirit of your mind; and that ye put on the new man, which after God is created in righteousness and true holiness. Wherefore putting away lying, speak every man truth with his neighbor: for we are members one of another. Be ye angry, and sin not: let not the sun go down upon your wrath: neither give place to the devil. Let him that stole steal no more: but rather let him labor, working with his hands the thing which is good, that he may have to give to him that needeth. Let no corrupt communication proceed out of your mouth, but that which is good to the use of edifying, that it may minister grace unto the hearers. And grieve not the Holy Spirit of God, whereby ye are sealed unto the day of redemption. Let all bitterness, and wrath, and anger, and clamor, and evil speaking, be put away from you, with all malice: and be ye kind one to another, tender-hearted, forgiving one another, even as God for Christ's sake hath forgiven you.

It is obvious that the renewed mind is free of bondage, past circumstances, habits, evil desires, and other self-defeating thinking, feelings, and behavior. It is also very obvious that whenever we read about the renewed mind in the Scriptures, we find that we are dealing with an urgent message to walk in love. To have the mind of Christ requires us to follow in his footsteps. In Ephesians 5:1, 2 we read: "Be ye therefore followers of God, as dear children; and walk in love, as Christ also hath loved us, and hath given himself for us an offering and a sacrifice to God for a sweetsmelling savor." It is only in such things as goodness, righteousness, forgiveness, truth, and other Christian attributes that we can have the fruit of the Spirit (Ephesians 4:25-32; 5:8, 9; Colossians 3:12-17; Galatians 5:22-26). It is also self-evident that we need rational minds. As we follow the program outlined in this book, we can eliminate much of our negative emotional behavior. Jesus was the most rational person that ever walked on earth. As his followers, it behooves us to be as rational as possible in all things.

While it is important to have as much self-control and self-direction as possible (rather than being directed by the whims and fancies of others), it is clear that victory in this life can only come to us by giving executive control of our minds to the Holy Spirit. We read in Zechariah 4:6: "Not by might, nor by power, but by my Spirit, saith the Lord of hosts." We can truly overcome the world if we believe in Jesus Christ as the Son of God (1 John 5:4, 5). More than that, we can be "fellow heirs" (Ephesians 3:6) with Christ, and come to understand the "mystery of Christ" (Ephesians 3:3, 4)—namely, that by faith he will live in our hearts (Ephesians 3:17). The fact that the kingdom of God is within us (Luke 17:21) is a blessing with great responsibility. However, God will help us to help ourselves if we follow his instructions:

Rejoice in the Lord always: and again I say, Rejoice. Let your moderation be known unto all men. The Lord is at hand. Be careful for nothing; but in every thing by prayer and supplication with thanksgiving let your requests be made known unto God. And the peace of God, which passeth all understanding, shall keep your hearts and minds through Christ Jesus. Finally, brethren, whatsoever things are true, whatsoever things are honest, whatsoever things are just, whatsoever things are pure, whatsoever things are lovely, whatsoever things are of good report; if there be any virtue, and if there be any praise, think on these things. Those things, which ye have both learned, and received, and heard, and seen in me, do: and the God of peace shall be with you. (Philippians 4:4-9)

The Apostle Paul makes it abundantly clear that we need to do something if we expect God to transform our lives. Clearly we need to be objective ("whatsoever things are true") and to think about our behavior ("think on these things"), to be rational in our dealings with others ("Let your moderation be known"). We need to do away with our old ways, and to follow those better ways which we have "learned, and received, and heard, and seen." To have a renewed mind, however, would be an impossibility except for the fact that God has provided a way; namely, "I can do all things, through Christ which strengtheneth me" (Philippians 4:13).

One thing we need to understand clearly is that the battle between good and evil, between the kingdom of Satan and the kingdom of God, is fought in our minds. There is an ongoing struggle between foolishness and wisdom, the negative and positive, the destructive and constructive, the carnal and spiritual, darkness and light, etc. However, our minds are not merely a battlefield; we are charged to direct the battle and will be held accountable for its outcome. We cannot be successful unless we understand both our strengths and weaknesses; we must know the forces on both sides of the struggle. It is certainly folly not to know as much as possible about the enemy that opposes us. Failure to understand the forces of evil and the consequences of giving any territory to them (by being asleep, allowing ourselves to be tricked, not making the necessary preparations, or whatever) is at the heart of all our problems and troubles. Certainly stupidity and ignorance will have to rank at the top of our list as primary causes for our difficulties.

An excellent way to prepare ourselves is to know something about the various minds that are described in the Scriptures. God tells us that we need to be victorious over the *reprobate, blinded, defiled, vain, doubtful,* and *carnal mind,* and to embrace only the *renewed mind.* By being aware of the forces that battle in our minds, we can better deal with them. Likewise, a greater understanding of the workings of our natural minds will enable us to make wiser choices in all of our thinking, feeling, and actions. Here are the minds God teaches us about:

The reprobate mind. This is the depraved mind that does not want to repent. It is truly the mind of the self-defeating, even self-destroying individual who does not care about the results of wickedness, now or later. This is what we read in Romans 1:28-32:

> And even as they did not like to retain God in their knowledge, God gave them over to a reprobate mind, to do those things which are not convenient; being filled with all unrighteousness, fornication, wickedness, covetousness, maliciousness; full of envy, murder, debate, deceit, malignity; whisperers, backbiters, haters of God, despiteful, proud, boasters, inventors of evil things, disobedient to parents, without understanding, covenant-breakers, without natural affection, implacable, unmerciful: who, knowing the judgment of God, that they which commit such things are worthy of death, not only do the same, but have pleasure in them that do them.

The blinded mind. Here we find a mind that is blinded to spiritual truth, unbelievers who cannot see the light although it is clearly shining. The blinded mind reminds us that we do not see with our eyes, and do not hear with our ears, but rather that we see and hear (if we are ready to do so) with our minds. We allow Satan to blind our minds with self-defeating and self-destructive thoughts, feelings, and actions that prevent us from seeing the truth. It is interesting to note that those who are in darkness want us to be in darkness also. The blinded mind can be face to face with miracles and not believe. This is what 2 Corinthians 4:3, 4 tells us about the blinded mind:

> But if our gospel be hid, it is hid to them that are lost: in whom the god of this world hath blinded the minds of them which believe not, lest the light of the glorious gospel of Christ, who is the image of God, should shine unto them.

The defiled mind. This is the unclean mind that has been placed under the control of Satan. The Scriptures tell us that we create our own behavior (Proverbs 16:9), and that evil comes from our own heart (Matthew 15:19). Consequently *we* are the ones who place ourselves under the control of Satan. It is not our environment, but our thinking (Proverbs 23:7) that makes us what we are. The Scriptures make it abundantly clear that we are responsible for our behavior and we will be held accountable for it. This is what we find in Mark 7:20-23 about the defiled mind:

> And he said, That which cometh out of the man, that defileth the man. For from within, out of the heart of men, proceed evil thoughts, adulteries, fornications, murders, thefts, covetousness, wickedness, deceit, lasciviousness, an evil eye, blasphemy, pride, foolishness: all these evil things come from within, and defile the man.

The vain mind. The vain mind is the mind that is wasting its time, for it is unproductive of worthwhile things. The vain mind may very well spend a great deal of time, money, and effort on many activities; however, there will be no constructive results. The work of the vain mind is fruitless, for the work is done in ignorance. Insensitive to the truth and concerned with greed and selfishness, it is an immoral mind. This is what the Scriptures tell us about the vain mind (Ephesians 4:17-19):

> This I say therefore, and testify in the Lord, that ye henceforth walk not as other Gentiles walk, in the vanity of their mind, having the understanding darkened, being alienated from the life of God through the ignorance that is in them, because of the blindness of their heart: who being past feeling have given themselves over unto lasciviousness, to work all uncleanness with greediness.

The doubtful mind. The doubtful mind is the mind that is uncertain. It is the mind of those who waver between one thing and another. The doubtful mind's lack of confidence is often reflected in suspicion and confusion. The doubtful mind lacks direction and will do one thing on one day and the opposite on the next, without knowing for sure if it is right to do so or not. The doubtful mind often tries to do contrary things—e.g., serve

God and mammon (Matthew 6:24). Since our mind is responsible for all of our actions, it is little wonder that the Scriptures
tell us that a double (doubtful) mind is reflected in everything
that we do (James 1:8). The renewed mind, one of faith and
obedience, knows what it wants and goes after it. The doubtful
mind, on the other hand, is perpetually mixed up. This is what
the Scriptures (James 1:5-8) teach us:

> If any of you lack wisdom, let him ask of God, that giveth to all
> men liberally, and upbraideth not; and it shall be given him. But
> let him ask in faith, nothing wavering: for he that wavereth is
> like a wave of the sea driven with the wind and tossed. For let
> not that man think that he shall receive any thing of the Lord.
> A double-minded man is unstable in all his ways.

The carnal mind. The carnal mind is the mind of the world.
It is the mind that concerns itself with temporal, material, and
unholy matters. The carnal mind is the sinful mind which is set
against God. The Scriptures tell us that as long as we participate in "envying, and strife, and division" (1 Corinthians 3:3)
we are still leading a worldly life. It is, of course, not possible to
be both carnal and spiritually minded at the same time. This is
what we find in Romans 8:5-8:

> For they that are after the flesh do mind the things of the flesh;
> but they that are after the Spirit, the things of the Spirit. For to
> be carnally minded is death; but to be spiritually minded is life
> and peace. Because the carnal mind is enmity against God: for
> it is not subject to the law of God, neither indeed can be. So
> then they that are in the flesh cannot please God.

The renewed mind. The renewed mind, as we have already
discussed, is the mind of Christ. It is the mind of forgiveness, of
peace, of love. It is the mind that will bring a transformed life
(Romans 12:2). The renewed mind is the spiritual mind, the
mind of Christ. It is the mind of "goodness and righteousness
and truth" (Ephesians 5:9). The renewed mind is Christ within
us (Luke 17:21; Colossians 1:27). It is the mind that provides
executive control over our body, mind, and spirit. Above all

things, it is a precious gift from God himself, as it is he who enables us to be "conformed to the image of his Son" (Romans 8:29). It is God who has chosen us and called us out of darkness (1 Peter 2:9) so that we may "walk in love, as Christ also hath loved us . . ." (Ephesians 5:2).

The renewed mind is seen in the ". . . new man, which after God is created in righteousness and true holiness" (Ephesians 4:24). The renewed mind has many beautiful attributes, such as being *sober* (Titus 2:6), *sound* (2 Timothy 1:7), *ready* (Acts 17:11), *humble* (Acts 20:19), *willing* (1 Chronicles 28:9), *pure* (2 Peter 3:1) and, of course, *spiritual* (Romans 8:6). When we meditate on these Scriptures, it becomes quickly evident that we need to prepare the vessel of our mind so that God can fill it to overflowing with his Spirit.

Whatever else we find as a reflection of the renewed mind, there is nothing that is more self-evident than the reflection of God's love. In 1 John 3:23, 24 we read: "And this is his commandment, That we should believe on the name of his Son Jesus Christ, and love one another, as he gave us commandment. And he that keepeth his commandments dwelleth in him, and he in him. And hereby we know that he abideth in us, by the Spirit which he hath given us."

In summary, the renewal of our natural mind is to be accomplished by us as we yield to the working of the Holy Spirit. God has given us the opportunity and the responsibility to lead lives that are pleasing to him. God has shown us that our minds are battle grounds between forces of good and evil. He has also shown us how we can successfully choose life or death. The renewed mind, however, is a *gift* of God to all who believe in— and follow—Jesus Christ as the Son of God. If we do not know Jesus Christ as our personal Savior, then we need to read the next chapter where we find God's simple plan of salvation.

And ye shall seek me, and find me, when ye shall search for me with all your heart. (Jeremiah 29:13)

13   Scriptural Steps to Salvation

Throughout this book we have emphasized that God calls us out of darkness, unhappiness, and sin, and everything that has to do with the carnal world. God has chosen us (John 15:16; 1 Peter 2:4) just as surely as he chose Abraham (Nehemiah 9:7). However, it is very important to understand that God will not force us to choose him. God calls us and touches our hearts, but he allows us a free choice (Deuteronomy 30:19, 20; Joshua 24:15; Isaiah 7:15).

It is essential that we have this free choice; for without it there is no freedom, growth, challenge, or responsibility. Opportunity comes with accountability.

God wants us happy and to make those choices that are in our best interest. Both believers and unbelievers are quick to agree that the source of happiness is love. The great misunderstanding, however, takes place when we fail to understand the true source of love. The Scriptures tell us that God is a Spirit (John 4:24) and that God is love (1 John 4:8). In fact, there is no description that more accurately tells us what love is than 1 Corinthians 13.

Charity [love] suffereth long, and is kind; charity vaunteth not itself, is not puffed up, doth not behave itself unseemly, seeketh

not her own, is not easily provoked, thinketh no evil; rejoiceth
not in iniquity, but rejoiceth in the truth; beareth all things,
believeth all things, hopeth all things, endureth all things.
(verses 4-7)

Many of us have difficulty in believing that there is a God,
and this difficulty is the result of the confusion that Satan has
spread in the world. We are, in fact, so confused that we do not
even bother to investigate. We do not take time to check out
the claims the Lord makes. We do not take time to read the
Scriptures, and to bring them to the test. No scientific claim is
ever treated so stupidly. Whenever there is a so-called new
scientific finding, we hurry to our laboratories or field settings
and investigate these findings. Why are so many of us afraid to
test whether or not God lives? Why are so many of us afraid to
find out that there is an all-knowing, all-powerful God who
does in fact know exactly what we need, and is ready and
willing to meet that need? Is it because we prefer not to know?
Is it because we are afraid? Are we afraid the price is too high?
Is it that we may have to give up certain things we hold dear
and near to our hearts, whether they are destructive or not?
There are many possible reasons why we often fail to check
into the claims that are made by God. Whatever the reason, it
is foolish to summarily dismiss the existence of a living, all-
loving, all-powerful, all-knowing God. For truly all of us are in
need of a great many answers and are looking for solutions to
problems. Most of us are concerned with the meaning of life.
Most of us are concerned about the purpose of living and
dying. Most of us are concerned about the continuation of our
existence. Most of us would like to live as happily and as long
as possible. In fact, we are so engrossed in the betterment of our
lives and trying to find out where we came from, where we are
going, and how we can survive as a human race that we spend
untold billions of dollars every year trying to control our
weight or find cures for diseases, ways to live longer, etc. We
also spend huge fortunes, energy, and time to study the intrica-
cies of the sex lives of insects, the behavior of monkeys and
rats, and thousands of different projects, virtually all of them
designed to make us happier as human beings.

In search of answers to our questions about life and death, we spend unbelievable amounts of time and money. We do so gladly and willingly, even sacrificially. Now, does it make any good sense not to investigate the claims made by God as described in the Scriptures? We can test the Scriptures without spending any money at all, without any kind of elaborate equipment, without having to do dangerous things, without any kind of harm or damage to our environment, without the assistance of other people. It is indeed incomprehensible that thinking people would not investigate the claims made by God.

Are we in search of happiness? God says he can provide it for us. Are we looking for guidance and solace? God maintains that he can help. Are we looking for healing of painful memories? Our anger? Our depressions? Our frustrations? Our illnesses? He tells us that he can help there too. Are we lonely? Alone? Isolated? He says he can help. Do we feel powerless, life holds no meaning? God says that he will remedy that. Do we need someone to help us to do anything and everything in our best interest? God says that can be done. His claims are great. Where is the proof? How can we find out? Simple!

However, there is one thing we need to understand in advance. Just as we cannot converse with people who do not speak our language, so it is with God. When we speak in English to a group of people who have never even heard that language, they are going to learn absolutely nothing. So it is with God. God speaks to us through the language of the Scriptures, and through the Holy Spirit. He tells us that we need faith to deal with him. We do not see him, yet we can find him. God tells us that we can have faith merely by hearing (listening to) his Word. All we need to do is read the Scriptures. If God exists, then by hearing his Word, we will receive faith (Romans 10:17).

But there is more. God tells us that we need to activate our faith, to step out in faith. Nothing comes from nothing, and unless we test our faith there is no use for this faith. God tells us that if we read the Scriptures, obtain faith, step out in faith, and follow his instructions, we will get the answers which we need. Once we are believers and followers, we shall be able to communicate with God via the Holy Spirit.

The Scriptures tell us something that is very important for us if we want to investigate the claims made by God. In 1 John 4:6 we read: "We are of God: he that knoweth God heareth us; he that is not of God heareth not us. . . ." But then we might say it would be impossible for all of us who do not believe in God ever to hear him. Not so, for God goes on to tell us that by loving him and others he will dwell in us *and* will give us his Spirit (1 John 4:13).

God has made it easy for us to know him. We are the ones who are making it difficult to know him, because of our lack of faith, our doubts, fears, greed, and selfishness.

God has shown us that he loves us by means of a plan. This is the plan of salvation. He has provided a simple plan, whereby we may have salvation, learn to speak with God, receive the Holy Spirit, and receive answers to all our questions! We may test whether or not he will do all the things that he promises us in the Scriptures. Here are the simple steps to salvation and total fulfillment:

WE MUST ACKNOWLEDGE OUR SINS

Even the most superfluous, rudimentary reflection and observation will tell us that we are sinners. God tells us that all human beings are imperfect, that all of us have sinned, and that no human being is righteous. The Bible says: "For all have sinned, and come short of the glory of God" (Romans 3:23). Knowing this, however, is not enough. Our relationship with God is always in an active sense. We need to do something. In this case, we need to admit to God that we are sinners. We might simply say, "God be merciful to me a sinner" (Luke 18:13).

WE MUST REPENT OF OUR SINS

Obviously it is of no value to admit that we are sinners, and leave it at that. We also need to regret sinful behavior. The admission of our sins is setting the stage for changing our ways. However, we only will change if we have true remorse. It is only when we give up our old self that we may have a new self. The Bible tells us, ". . . except ye repent, ye shall all likewise perish" (Luke 13:3). In Acts 3:19 we read: "Repent ye therefore, and be converted, that your sins may be blotted out." We must have regret and *do* something about this regret. After that we can start a new life.

WE MUST CONFESS OUR SINS
God tells us in the Scriptures that words are all-important to success or failure, to health or disease. It is simply not possible to have things go right unless we think and speak right. God wants us to remove the sinful burdens from our heart and to leave us filled with happiness. In 1 John 1:9 we read: "If we confess our sins, he is faithful and just to forgive us our sins, and to cleanse us from all unrighteousness." As soon as we believe, we must act on our belief. Only when we do this can we receive the reward. The Scriptures tell us, ". . . if thou shalt confess with thy mouth the Lord Jesus, and shalt believe in thine heart that God hath raised him from the dead, thou shalt be saved" (Romans 10:9).

WE MUST FORSAKE OUR SINS
It is obvious that it is not possible to engage in sinful and nonsinful behavior at the same time. It is equally obvious that we must reject evil before we can accept goodness. Only good thoughts will give us good feelings. All good and all evil things come out of our heart. The Scriptures tell us exactly what we need to do. In Isaiah 55:7 we read, "Let the wicked forsake his way, and the unrighteous man his thoughts: and let him return unto the Lord . . . for he will abundantly pardon."

WE MUST BELIEVE IN JESUS
We only act on the thoughts we believe. We can have thoughts about a great number of things, but only those thoughts that we really believe will result in action. Only if we believe in Jesus Christ as the Son of God, as the promised Savior, can we have the benefits of his sacrifice of love. The Scriptures make it very clear, and Christians intimately know, that God is a God of love. In John 3:16 we find the clearest description of that love: "For God so loved the world that he gave his only begotten Son, that whosoever believeth in him should not perish, but have everlasting life."

WE MUST RECEIVE JESUS INTO OUR HEART

Only when we truly make Jesus a part of ourselves shall we receive his power.

In John 1:11, 12 we read, "He came unto his own, and his own received him not. But as many as received him, to them gave he power to become the sons of God, even to them that believe on his name."

AND NOT OVERLOOK BAPTISM

The Scriptures show that belief in Jesus Christ and accepting him are more important than anything else we can do. It is more important than any outward acts or any kind of physical or material thing. The Scriptures tell us that we are saved by "grace . . . through faith" (Ephesians 2:8). However, there are also many Scriptures that emphasize the importance of baptism. In fact, in one Scripture verse it is listed along with believing in the Lord. In Mark 16:16 the Lord himself says: "He that believeth and is baptized shall be saved; but he that believeth not shall be damned." Yet, we are saved by blood and not by water. In Hebrews 9:22 we read: ". . . without the shedding of blood is no remission." It is very clear that we should be baptized *after* we have been saved. Perhaps nothing makes the importance of baptism more obvious than the fact that Jesus himself was baptized by John the Baptist (Matthew 3:13-16), and many Scriptures throughout the New Testament remind us to follow Jesus in baptism. (See Chapter 15 for references.)

These are the simple scriptural steps to salvation and eternal happiness. By following these steps in faith, we receive our salvation—that is, our deliverance from the consequences of sin. We are then redeemed by the blood of Christ. Jesus refers to this as being "born again" (John 3:3). Our salvation hinges on a free choice that God has given to us. He has touched our hearts even as we read these words. He has called us out, and waits for our response. It makes no difference who we are or what we have done; God wants to make us his children. All we need to do is to make a decision. (Salvation is first a decision and only later a feeling.) If we choose life over death, joy over despair, the power of love and eternal life, then we need to pray a simple prayer, perhaps something like this:

Dear God, I know that I am a sinner. I believe that Jesus died and shed his blood for my sins.

I now receive Jesus into my heart as my personal Lord and Savior, and I will confess him before others. Thank you, God, for setting me free and making me your child. Amen.

Once we have prayed this prayer, we need to tell others, so that all of God's promises will come true. In Matthew we read, "Whosoever therefore shall confess me before men, him will I confess also before my Father which is in heaven" (Matthew 10:32). The scriptural steps to salvation are simple: we realize our sinful existence, repent, forsake our wicked ways, confess our sins to God, believe that he forgives us, and tell others about the wonderful things that the Lord is doing to us, as is written in Mark 5:19, "Go home to thy friends, and tell them what great things the Lord hath done for thee."

To be a Christian is a wonderful thing. It is a great joy to know that we are God's children. However, for continued growth and to receive numerous powerful blessings from the Lord, we need to follow his instructions for everything in our lives.

For they [my words] are life unto those that find them, and health to all their flesh. (Proverbs 4:22)

14   Scriptural Steps to Happiness

Happiness is defined in a great number of ways by a great number of people. However, there seems to be general agreement that happiness usually involves a feeling of contentment, comfort, and peace. God tells us that we are happy if we—among other things—find wisdom (Proverbs 3:13), have mercy on the poor (Proverbs 14:21), trust in him (Proverbs 16:20), keep the law (Proverbs 29:18), listen to him (Job 5:17), and do not condemn (Romans 14:22). The highest degree of happiness, namely "joy," is found by those who "walk in the Spirit" (Galatians 5:16, 22).

If we wish to become happy, we simply need to follow the advice the Lord has given us. He tells us that we will get what we give. As we give happiness to others, we will receive happiness in return. Once we truly start to reach out to others, our unhappiness will start to disappear. This is what the Lord tells us in Luke 6:38:

> Give, and it shall be given unto you; good measure, pressed down, and shaken together, and running over, shall men give into your bosom. For with the same measure that ye mete withal it shall be measured to you again.

The scriptural prescription for happiness is clear: reach out and give happiness, and you will receive happiness. In fact, it is not possible to be happy if we are self-centered, or greedy, or totally wrapped up in and with ourselves, or if we isolate ourselves in other ways from people. Happiness, yes, even "life" and "health," are found in God's Word (Proverbs 4:20-22). If we follow the instructions from his Word, we will find true and lasting happiness. Here are ten scriptural steps to happiness:

Rx FOR HAPPINESS

Praise God from morning till night.
Do this when you first awake and let it be the last thing you do before falling asleep.

> O praise the Lord, all ye nations: praise him, all ye people. For his merciful kindness is great toward us: and the truth of the Lord endureth forever. Praise ye the Lord. (Psalm 117)

Thank God for all of your blessings.
"The blessing of the Lord, it maketh rich." (Proverbs 10:22)

Our greatest blessing is the Lord himself. Consider your blessings as a child of God. Don't overlook the vast number of blessings, starting perhaps with your freedom, clothing, shelter, food. But pay even more attention to nonmaterial blessings such as the opportunity to worship God, to attend church, to share the gospel, to extend a hand to someone else.

Never equate human beings with their behavior.
You see only a small portion of all their behaviors. Do not place a global rating of bad or good on a person merely because you see or want to see certain things. All human beings are fallible. None of us is perfect. None of us are in a position to judge. Daily remind yourself that you are fallible, and so is everyone else.

Refuse to complain, whine, gripe, blame, or feel sorry for yourself.

If you want to feel bad, merely remind yourself and others how things "always" go wrong for you; how "no one" loves you; how you "never" seem to do anything right; etc.

You must steadfastly refuse to participate in gripe sessions, pity get-togethers, or those very destructive meetings where you can "discuss" other people. Be mindful of the following:

> Let no corrupt communication proceed out of your mouth, but that which is good to the use of edifying, that it may minister grace unto the hearers. (Ephesians 4:29)

Your feelings are the results of your thoughts (the ones you believe!) "For as he thinketh in his heart, so is he" (Proverbs 23:7).

To feel good, you need to think good. Listen to this:

> Let all bitterness and wrath, and anger, and clamor, and evil speaking, be put away from you, with all malice: and be ye kind one to another, tender-hearted, forgiving one another, even as God for Christ's sake hath forgiven you. (Ephesians 4:31, 32)

Do your daily tasks, even if you don't feel like doing them.
You may tell yourself that you cannot do them; and because feelings result from what we tell ourselves, it is only logical, natural, and normal that you do not feel up to the things you have said that you cannot do. To make it easier for us to do our routine, daily tasks, we can make a simple schedule. Then we follow the schedule every day, and we listen to the schedule (our own thoughts really) rather than to our moods.

> Whatsoever thy hand findeth to do, do it with thy might. (Ecclesiastes 9:10)

> Trust in the Lord with all thine heart; and lean not unto thine own understanding. In all thy ways acknowledge him, and he shall direct thy paths. (Proverbs 3:5, 6)

Accept your limitations.

Simply learn to accept the fact that all of us have certain limitations. Some more, some less. Some more today, others less today. Some less today and more tomorrow. It is utter folly to compare yourself to others. If you do not seem as quick as others, or do not seem to remember everything as well as others, then simply accept this as objective reality. If you can correct or improve on the situation, all the better. If you cannot, then this is just one more demonstration of human fallibility. A C student is not the same as a C person. A slow person is not the same as a sinner. A quick person is not the same as a good person.

No human being is perfect. Because all human beings are fallible, and their "fortunes" change daily, it is clear that all of them have limitations, conflicts, problems, failings, difficulties, etc.

Whenever you exaggerate something (magnify beyond the truth), you are liable to feel excessively sorry for yourself. By saying that you cannot do anything (when the truth is that there are some things you do very well, others you do not do very well, and again others that you do poorly), you are not only untruthful, you are also going to feel bad. Likewise, if you tell yourself that other human beings have no limitations, you are simply lying to yourself. The truth is that all human beings have all kinds of limitations—even if you are not necessarily aware of most of them.

Stop comparing yourself to others. Stop whining and complaining about your limitations. Correct what you can, and accept the rest. There are people (many, many people) who have no hands, but they make beautiful paintings with their mouth. Just as the blind, the deaf, and others with serious limitations can and do overcome these limitations in many ways, so can you. Likewise, just as they accept what cannot be changed, so can you.

Have compassion for others, but not overconcern.

Don't make the mistake of confusing your overconcern with positive behavior on your part. The truth is that overconcern rarely accomplishes anything at all, except, of course, that we have one more problem (our unhappiness). If your friend breaks a leg, you will very unlikely go out and break a leg so that you can show your concern. So why do you so often immobilize yourself mentally trying to carry the burdens of others? You can help others far better if you are concerned, rather than overconcerned. Show compassion in a constructive way. Compassion is expressed in positive deeds. If you want to help the poor, donate food, time, clothes, or money. Your tears do little for them.

One very important thing you can do (a positive, constructive deed) is to be a good model of a reasonable person. This means that you will think, feel, and act (start with the thinking, the rest follows!) in objective—that is, truthful—ways. It also means that you do only those things which are life- and health-preserving, and bring no sadness or harm of any kind to your loved ones, or do anything that will separate you in any way from God. It is the will of God that you love him, and others as yourself.

Just as it is not very constructive to have overconcern for others, it is also not good to have overconcern for yourself. Listen to this:

> Therefore take no thought, saying, What shall we eat? or, What shall we drink? or, Wherewithal shall we be clothed? (For after all these things do the Gentiles seek:) for your heavenly Father knoweth that ye have need of all these things. But seek ye first the kingdom of God, and his righteousness; and all these things shall be added unto you. Take therefore no thought for the morrow: for the morrow shall take thought for the things of itself. Sufficient unto the day is the evil thereof. (Matthew 6:31-34)

Make a simple list and schedule those things that have been left undone for some time.
In addition to having a list of your daily routine tasks, it may be helpful to have a listing of things that have been overlooked in the past. Place them in some order of priority and begin tackling them, one at a time. While you do all this, continue to

praise God, thank him for his blessings, and concentrate on your love for God, God's love for you, and your love for others. Always be mindful of your status as a child of God, and of the fact that you are very important to him and fully acceptable to him because you are doing his will. Never forget that you have a very important mission, purpose, and goal, and that is to be a witness to the Lord. You have all the meaning in your life that you could possibly need by allowing the Lord to work through you. Thus, you need to be a light for others, and a reasonable person. Be mindful of the words of the Apostle Paul: "I beseech you therefore, brethren, by the mercies of God, that ye present your bodies a living sacrifice, holy, acceptable unto God, which is your reasonable service" (Romans 12:1).

To do the things that need to be done, you may well need a list, but never overlook the #1 priority of taking care of yourself. The things you eat and drink, your sleep, exercise, fresh air, etc. are very important!

Quit blaming yourself.
It is very important that you quit blaming yourself for real or imagined failures. You cannot undo the past by lamenting all the things you wish you had or had not done. Much of your self-blame is directly related to anger with yourself. You are frequently given to demanding and insisting, rather than wanting and wishing. Much of your anger is the result of demanding that things should have been different for you. However, objective reality will show you that whatever happened should have happened. The things we have done in the past should have happened, for we often walked in darkness. Frequently we were too stupid, too ignorant, or too disturbed to have done any better. Also, we may have been unwilling to do the things that would have been better for us. Whatever the reason, all human beings are fallible and therefore all human beings have made and/or are making mistakes.

As for your sins, God is willing to forgive them if you are willing to confess them. "He that covereth his sins shall not prosper: but whoso confesseth and forsaketh them shall have mercy" (Proverbs 28:13). God is willing to forgive your sins. Are you? Or are you superhuman? Perhaps even above God?

Then why would you not forgive yourself after God has done so? God wants us to confess our sins, forsake them, and make restitution whenever and wherever possible. God especially wants us to forgive others, just as he has forgiven us. Listen to what Jesus has to say on this: "For if ye forgive men their trespasses, your heavenly Father will also forgive you: but if you forgive not men their trespasses, neither will your Father forgive your trespasses" (Matthew 6:14, 15).

Extend yourself beyond yourself.
The moment you reach out to others, unhesitatingly and fully caring, the Lord will bless you. Strange as it may seem to you, there are literally millions of people who are in need of your help, and who will gladly accept your help. Never lie to yourself and tell yourself that there is nothing, or no one, to live for. There are countless people who need your love, your hand, your smile, your care. Visit someone; call someone up; think about the old, the sick, the poor, the lonely, the grief-stricken, etc. Call or see someone, not to complain, not to receive solace for your problems, but to give them something of yourself. See what you can do for them. People everywhere desperately need your help. Always work hard to be a good model for others, and look for ways by which you can extend yourself beyond your own cares and concerns.

The secret of true happiness ("the peace of God") is found in *prayer, praise,* and *thanksgiving,* as we read in Philippians 4:4-7:

> Rejoice in the Lord always: and again I say, Rejoice. Let your moderation be known unto all men. The Lord is at hand. Be careful for nothing; but in every thing by prayer and supplication with thanksgiving let your requests be made known unto God. And the peace of God, which passeth all understanding, shall keep your hearts and minds through Christ Jesus.

It is clear that prayer is the key to everything. It is in prayer that we communicate with God. He has made it abundantly clear that he will hear our prayers. Millions of people, even today, can testify to this. Here are some very important Scriptures on prayer:

If my people, which are called by my name, shall humble themselves, and pray, and seek my face, and turn from their wicked ways; then will I hear from heaven, and will forgive their sin, and will heal their land. (2 Chronicles 7:14)

Thou hast given him his heart's desire, and hast not withholden the requests of his lips. (Psalm 21:2)

The righteous cry, and the Lord heareth, and delivereth them out of all their troubles. (Psalm 34:17)

Delight thyself also in the Lord; and he shall give thee the desires of thine heart. Commit thy way unto the Lord; trust also in him; and he shall bring it to pass. (Psalm 37:4, 5)

And call upon me in the day of trouble: I will deliver thee, and thou shalt glorify me. (Psalm 50:15)

As for me, I will call upon God; and the Lord shall save me. Evening, and morning, and at noon, will I pray, and cry aloud: and he shall hear my voice. (Psalm 55:16, 17)

In the day of my trouble I will call upon thee: for thou wilt answer me. (Psalm 86:7)

The sacrifice of the wicked is an abomination to the Lord: but the prayer of the upright is his delight. (Proverbs 15:8)

And it shall come to pass, that before they call, I will answer; and while they are yet speaking, I will hear. (Isaiah 65:24)

And ye shall seek me, and find me, when ye shall search for me with all your heart. (Jeremiah 29:13)

Call unto me, and I will answer thee, and show thee great and mighty things, which thou knowest not. (Jeremiah 33:3)

But I say unto you, Love your enemies, bless them that curse you, do good to them that hate you, and pray for them which despitefully use you, and persecute you. (Matthew 5:44)

Ask, and it shall be given you; seek, and ye shall find; knock, and it shall be opened unto you: for every one that asketh receiveth; and he that seeketh findeth; and to him that knocketh it shall be opened. (Matthew 7:7, 8)

Again I say unto you, That if two of you shall agree on earth as touching any thing that they shall ask, it shall be done for them of my Father which is in heaven. For where two or three are gathered together in my name, there am I in the midst of them. (Matthew 18:19, 20)

And all things, whatsoever ye shall ask in prayer, believing, ye shall receive. (Matthew 21:22)

Therefore I say unto you, What things soever ye desire, when ye pray, believe that ye receive them, and ye shall have them. And when ye stand praying, forgive, if ye have aught against any; that your Father also which is in heaven may forgive you your trespasses. But if ye do not forgive, neither will your Father which is in heaven forgive your trespasses. (Mark 11:24-26)

For every one that asketh receiveth; and he that seeketh findeth; and to him that knocketh it shall be opened. (Luke 11:10)

If ye abide in me, and my words abide in you, ye shall ask what ye will, and it shall be done unto you. (John 15:7)

If ye shall ask any thing in my name, I will do it. (John 14:14)

But we will give ourselves continually to prayer, and to the ministry of the word. (Acts 6:4)

But without faith it is impossible to please him: for he that cometh to God must believe that he is, and that he is a rewarder of them that diligently seek him. (Hebrews 11:6)

And this is the confidence that we have in him, that, if we ask any thing according to his will, he heareth us: and if we know that he hear us, whatsoever we ask, we know that we have the petitions that we desired of him. (1 John 5:14, 15)

PRAISE GOD!

Again I say unto you, That if two of you shall agree on earth as touching any thing that they shall ask, it shall be done for them of my Father which is in heaven. For where two or three are gathered together in my name, there am I in the midst of them.
(Matthew 18:19, 20)

15 How to Start a Christian Self-Help Group

It is very easy to start a Christian self-help group. All that we need to do is find one or two Christians and we have a Christian group. What is more, we have the promise of the Lord that he himself will be in our midst and will grant us the desires of our heart. Of course, as Christians we are acutely aware that all our help comes from the Lord. In our particular groups we emphasize *self-help* for several reasons. We are to be distinguished from professional groups and overreliance on other people to solve our problems. If there is one outstanding quality in our groups, it is the recognition that only *a difference in our thinking* will make *a difference in the quality of our lives*. Even where it concerns physical problems, we need first of all a change in our thinking. We need to recognize that we are responsible for ourselves physically, mentally, and spiritually.

The Scriptures remind us of two very important things: that we must look to God for help, "for vain is the help of man" (Psalm 60:11); and that we must actively do certain things for ourselves. Whatever these things are, there is always the element of personal choice. All good things come from God and all evil things come from Satan, but the choice of one or the other comes from us. That is the power, the opportunity, and the responsibility with which God has entrusted us. He tells us to choose whom we will serve (Joshua 24:15), and encourages us to make the right choices. He shows us that it is better for us to choose life over death (Deuteronomy 30:19); good over evil (Isaiah 7:15); a renewed mind over a doubtful (Luke 12:29, 31), blinded (2 Corinthians 4:4), defiled (Titus 1:15), or reprobate mind (Romans 1:28-32).

We read in the Scriptures that God has chosen us (John 15:16). However, he tells us that we must do something to get the benefits of that choice. Jesus tells us that whatsoever we "ask" we will receive (John 15:16). In fact, that is the message throughout the Scriptures. While we have been chosen (1 Peter 2:4), just as God chose Abraham (Nehemiah 9:7), we still have the full responsibility and freedom to accept or reject his love, and to seek out wisdom or foolishness (Ecclesiastes 7:25). God has already helped us, he has already done everything that needs to be done. The Lord loved us and died for us "while we were yet sinners" (Romans 5:8). God has helped us throughout the ages. He is the source of all our strength. With the Psalmist we cry, "make haste to help me" (Psalm 40:13), for we know that God is our help and shield (Psalm 115:9).

Christian self-help is helping ourselves, and one another, to Christian self-enhancement. Not for self-deification, but to the glory of God. Christian self-help means doing the will of God—that is, to love God, others, and ourselves. Self-help does not mean that we are sufficient to ourselves, for we are not (1 John 1:10). It does mean that we emphasize the work that *we* must do, rather than the work we expect others to do for us. Sound advice and good information only becomes of value if we are ready, able, and willing to use it in the self-counseling process. Christian self-help groups may teach us various ways by which we may become more able, ready, and willing to do that which only we can do for ourselves.

We have no competition with professional people. In fact, we are grateful for the good work that so many of them are doing. We encourage professionals to serve all people unselfishly with true dedication and love. Christian self-help groups are no substitution for professional help, as clearly there is a useful and necessary function for both professional help and self-help. Many a person who has had professional help, of whatever kind—be it pastoral, medical, psychological, financial, social, or whatever else—can greatly benefit by participation in self-help groups. Likewise, those of us who are not benefiting by self-help or self-help groups need to seek professional help without delay.

While it is very simple to start a Christian self-help group, it is nevertheless sound wisdom to establish some guidelines. The following are some suggestions we may wish to incorporate in our group rules. Again, this is a recommended format, and we may well want to rewrite them to suit our particular needs.

SUGGESTED FORMAT
FOR CHRISTIAN SELF-HELP GROUPS

As an example, The Middle City Church Christian Self-Help Group is a nonprofit, voluntary association of people which meets regularly to study and practice self-counseling methods within a Christian framework.

The chief purpose of our group is to teach one another how to reduce unwanted painful emotions such as anxiety, guilt, anger, and depression, and to increase desirable emotions such as serenity, joy, love, and enthusiasm. The overall purpose of our group is to help ourselves to greater physical, mental, and spiritual health. We believe that the application of Christian principles and objective thinking will enable us to get along more comfortably and effectively with others, to grow in the Christian faith, and to lead more effective Christian lives.

Through the study and application of objective thinking methods, and a faithful study and application of the Scriptures, we believe that we will gain increased insights into our thinking, feeling, and behavior. We believe that we are primarily the end-product of our thinking, and that only a difference in our thinking will make a difference in the quality of our lives.

By accepting responsibility for our actions, by choosing wisely, by gaining a deeper understanding of our thinking, emotions, and actions, and above all by the grace of God, we are increasing our knowledge of God, of others and of ourselves. We follow the admonition of the Apostle Paul, who warns, ". . . be not conformed to this world: but be ye transformed by the renewing of your mind, that ye may prove what is that good, and acceptable, and perfect will of God" (Romans 12:2).

We believe that there are a great number of people who are in need of physical, spiritual, and emotional self-help methods, and we open our group to those people without regard to ethnic, social, cultural, or religious backgrounds. We are a Christ-centered group, and we will not deny our caring and sharing to anyone. We recognize that self-defeating thoughts, feelings, and actions, irresponsibility, failure to listen to God's perfect guidance, and many other such reasons are the main causes for many of our difficulties.

Consequently we seek to follow objective means to resolve our difficulties with God's help, as promised us in his Word.

We have resolved to meet every Tuesday at 7 P.M., in the Middle City Church, under the leadership of a member of that church. However, it is recognized that any qualified person may be the leader of our group. We believe that the qualification of the group leader is best determined by the group members. We have no professional qualifications for group leaders, except ability to do the required work and commitment to Jesus Christ, the ultimate Head of our group.

We specifically follow these guidelines:

(1) Our group is not a substitution for professional help, nor is it subservient to any professional person and/or professional group.

(2) Each member joins voluntarily, and is under no obligation to participate.

(3) No group member is under any obligation to the group leader or to the group members, except that everyone who attends must and will uphold the highest standards of Christian ethics while attending the group.

(4) Whenever a group member is not benefiting from self-help methods, that member must seek professional assistance without delay.

(5) It is understood, and accepted, that it is the sole responsibility of each individual member to determine whether or not to join our group, and when to discontinue our group.

(6) Our group is of a nonprofessional nature. We are a lay teaching self-help group. Mental health and other professionals may belong to our group as members, but will not have a special function or special privileges.

(7) The group leader and/or group members will refrain from giving medical, psychological, or other professional advice.

(8) The group leader will ensure at all times that members refrain from belaboring the past, complaining about others (present or absent), or blaming things, events, persons, etc., for their present predicament. Instead, the emphasis will consistently be on what we can do today about our thinking, feelings, and actions that will help us to lead more effective, efficient, and happier lives. What can we do, with God's help, to become physically, mentally, and spiritually healthier and happier?

(9) Our meetings are restricted to teaching objective thinking principles, and the application of God's Word, which will enable each of us to make the best possible choices for ourselves.

(10) There are no paid officers or directors in our group.

(11) No records are made of any kind.

(12) There is never any charge for attending our group.

(13) We are self-governing and self-sustaining, owing allegiance only to the Lord Jesus Christ.

(14) We encourage others to form similar groups, and we invite others to attend our group.

(15) We realize that our group functions most efficiently when all of us have at least a basic knowledge of some helpful literature, and especially of the Scriptures. Newcomers to our group will benefit most quickly by reading the Scriptures and some appropriate self-help books.

(16) While our group places no restriction on membership, it is understood that we are Christ-centered and that we must function within the particular structure of the church in which we meet, and that we uphold the Scriptures as final authority.

(17) Meeting in this church is a special privilege granted to us; however, this privilege may be withdrawn without advance notification and without explanation.

(18) All who attend our meetings must agree to abide by all of the rules as a condition of membership.

Hopefully, this *suggested* format will be of some help to those who desire to start a Christian self-help group. There are obviously many ways by which this may be accomplished. Christian self-help means helping ourselves with the help of God. Being in Christian self-help groups, however, also means unselfishly wanting to help others. We know from the Scriptures, and from observation and our personal lives, that human beings are both fallible and selfish. Yet, we are commanded to love others just as we love ourselves. Throughout this book we have stressed the importance of loving others. As soon as we extend ourselves beyond ourselves, some beautiful things start to happen. In Christian self-help groups there will be an overriding desire to help others, believers and unbelievers alike. We need to understand that as Christians our concern for the welfare of others has to outweigh our concern for self.

POSTSCRIPT

The end of this chapter is also the end of this book. Fortunately, the real content of this book has no ending. Hopefully the reading of it has helped us in some way to enhance our lives. Of course, there is no such thing on this earth as a "finished" human being. We frequently hear remarks about mature people, healthy personalities, etc.; however, all these merely describe ideals. Total victory will only come at the end of our lives, which need to be so ordered that we are ready to claim this victory at any moment.

Our lives may be seen as journeys to the top of a mountain. As we progress through life, our visions will increase and our enjoyments will multiply as we climb higher and higher. However, there are no easy mountain paths, there are no shortcuts, there are no long rest stops, and there is no turning back on the narrow road. However, we can see the mountaintop and we can anticipate our reward. The precious victory of eternal life awaits all believers, regardless of who we are and where we are at this very moment. However, none of us really knows the mountain; none of us really has all of the skills, strength, and stamina to reach the top. Without an experienced and caring guide, none of us can reach the top, and all of us are doomed to failure. However, there is a guide who will lead us to victory. He is calling to all who are lost, searching, lonely, isolated, and in trouble of whatever kind. Unfortunately far too many of us believe that we are self-sufficient, or that we do not get a fair deal out of the relationship. Self-sufficiency to the point of self-deification is the greatest of all illusions that we have created in our foolish minds. The one and only guide who can lead us to victory, who can bring us to the mountaintop, is the Lord Jesus Christ. He is the only guide who is all-knowing, all-powerful, always present, always existing, and all-loving! As a good guide and shepherd, he is calling out to us, "I lead the way; follow me."

To be sure that Jesus Christ is our guide, we need to answer his call. He needs to know that we accept his offer. We need to believe in our Guide, and we need to tell him that. No longer does the struggle to the mountaintop hold any terror, for we have the promise of God: "For God so loved the world, that he gave his only begotten Son, that whosoever believeth in him should not perish, but have everlasting life" (John 3:16).

May the peace and the joy of our Lord Jesus Christ rest upon us. May he guide us and protect us throughout our life's journey, and may we all reach that glorious mountaintop. Amen.

Thy word is a lamp unto my feet, and a light unto my path.
(Psalm 119:105)

16 Scriptural References for Self and Group Counseling

Abortion: Psa. 139:13-16; Isa. 43:1; 44:2, 24; 49:1, 5; 64:8; Jer. 1:5.

Adultery: Prov. 6:26, 32; Mal. 3:5; Matt. 5:28; 15:19; Heb. 13:4.

Affliction: Psa. 34:19; 119:67, 71, 75; 145:14; Prov. 24:10; Isa. 43:2; Rom. 8:28; 2 Cor. 1:4; 4:17, 18; Heb. 4:15, 16; 1 Pet. 5:6, 7.

Alcoholism: Prov. 20:1; 23:20, 21; 31:4, 6; Isa. 5:11; Luke 21:34; Rom. 13:13; Gal. 5:19-21.

Anger: Psa. 27:9; Prov. 14:17; 15:1; 22:24; 29:22; Matt. 5:22; Eph. 4:26, 31; Col. 3:8

Anxiety: Psa. 34:17; 55:22; Prov. 16:3; Isa. 26:3; 43:2; Matt. 6:25-34; Luke 21:34; Phil. 4:6, 7; Heb. 13:5; 1 Pet. 5:6, 7.

Babbling: Prov. 23:29; Ecc. 10:11; Acts 17:18; 1 Tim. 6:20; 2 Tim. 2:16.

Backsliding: 2 Chron. 30:9; Psa. 32:1-5; Prov. 11:20; 14:14; Isa. 44:22; 49:14-16; 57:15-18; Jer. 2:19; 3:12-15, 22; 18:1-6; Luke 15:4-7; 2 Pet. 2:20, 21.

Baptism: Matt. 3:13-16; 28:19; John 3:5; Acts 2:38, 41; 8:36-39; 10:47; 22:16; Rom. 6:3, 4; Gal. 3:26, 27; Col. 2:11, 12.

Bible, the: Deut. 12:28; Josh. 1:7-9; Psa. 119:11, 18, 105; Prov. 4:20-22; Isa. 55:11; Matt. 4:4; 5:18; Mark 13:31; John 5:39; Rom. 15:4; 2 Tim. 2:15; 3:16; 2 Pet. 1:21; Rev. 1:3; 22:18, 19.

Born again: John 1:12, 13; 3:3-7; 1 Pet. 1:22, 23; 1 John 5:4.

Burdens: Psa. 55:22; Gal. 6:2.

Chastening: Job 5:17; Psa. 94:12, 13; 119:67, 71; Prov. 3:11, 12; 1 Cor. 11:32; Heb. 12:5, 6; Rev. 3:19.

Choosing: Deut. 30:19; Josh. 24:15; Isa. 7:15; 56:4.

Children: Deut. 12:28; Psa. 103:17, 18; Prov. 11:21; 22:6; 23:13, 14; Eph. 6:1-4; Col. 3:20, 21.

Death: Psa. 23:4; 116:15; Ecc. 12:7; Isa. 57:1, 2; Luke 16:19-31; Acts 7:59; 1 Thess. 4:13-18; Rev. 14:13.

Depression: Psa. 9:9, 10; 31:22-24; 34:18; 37:5; 40:1, 2; 42:5, 11; 81:10; 103:1-5; 146:8; Isa. 35:3, 4; 50:10; Jer. 29:11-13; Zeph. 3:17; John 10:10; Rom. 5:5; 8:31; 12:12; Heb. 12:12, 13.

Discouragement: 2 Chron. 15:7; Psa. 27:14; 37:23, 24; 42:5, 11; 138:8; Prov. 24:16; Isa. 40:31; 50:7; Matt. 11:28-30; 1 Cor. 15:58; Gal. 6:9; 2 Thess. 3:13; 2 Tim. 1:7; Heb. 4:15, 16; Jas. 4:8.

Disease: Deut. 28:15, 22, 27, 28, 35, 45, 59-61; Gal. 3:13.

Divorce: Lev. 21:14; Num. 30:9; Jer. 3:8; Matt. 5:32; 19:3-9; 1 Cor. 7:10-17, 20, 24.

Enemies: Exod. 14:14; Psa. 18:47, 48; 56:9; 60:12; Prov. 24:17, 18; Isa. 41:10-13; 50:7-9; Jer. 20:11; 39:17, 18; Matt. 5:43-46; Luke 6:27-37; 23:34; Acts 7:60; Rom. 12:14, 19-21.

Envy: Psa. 37:1; 73:3; Prov. 24:1, 19; 2 Cor. 12:20; Gal. 5:21; 1 Tim. 6:4; Titus 3:3.

Eternal life: John 3:15, 16, 36; 6:40, 47; 10:27-29; 1 John 2:25; 5:11.

Evil: Psa. 23:4; 91:10; Amos 5:14; Rom. 12:17; 1 Thess. 5:15; Titus 3:2; 1 Pet. 3:9.

Faith: Matt. 8:23-26; 9:20-22, 27-30; 14:25-31; 15:21-28; 17:20; Mark 5:24-34; 9:23; 11:20-24; Luke 17:11-19; 18:35-43; Acts 14:8-10; Rom. 1:17; 10:17; 12:3; 2 Cor. 5:7; Gal. 3:11; Heb. 10:38; 11:1, 6 (read whole chapter); 12:1, 2; Jas. 1:2-7; 5:15; 1 Pet. 1:7, 8; 1 John 5:4.

False doctrines: Prov. 16:25; Mark 13:21-23; Gal. 1:8; Col. 2:8; 1 Tim. 4:1-3; 2 Pet. 2:1, 2; 1 John 4:1-3.

Fasting: 2 Sam. 12:15-23; 2 Chron. 20:1-3; Ezra 8:21-23; Jon. 3:1-10; Matt. 4:2; 6:16-18; 17:21.

Fear: Deut. 31:8; Psa. 23:4; 27:1-6; 34:4; 56:11; 57:3; 112:1, 7; 118:6; 121:7, 8; Prov. 1:33; Isa. 35:3, 4; 41:10; 43:5; 45:2, 3; 51:12, 13; Rom. 8:15; 2 Tim. 1:7; Heb. 13:5, 6; 1 Pet. 3:12, 13; 1 John 4:18.

Forgiveness: Psa. 85:2; 86:5; 103:3, 12; Isa. 1:18; 43:25; Matt. 6:14, 15; 18:21, 22; Mark 11:25, 26; Luke 17:3, 4; Eph. 4:32; Col. 2:13; 3:12, 13; Heb. 8:12; 10:17; 1 John 1:9.

Giving: Deut. 15:9-11; Prov. 3:9, 10; 11:24, 25; 19:17; 21:13; 28:27; Matt. 2:10, 11; 6:1-4; Luke 6:38; Rom. 12:8; 1 Cor. 16:1, 2; 2 Cor. 9:6-12.

Gladness: Psa. 4:7; 16:9; 30:11; 31:7; 64:10; 100:2; Heb. 1:9.

Guilt: Psa. 31:22; Isa. 44:22; 54:4-10; Rom. 7:18-25; 8:1, 2; 14:22; Heb. 10:17.

Hatred: Lev. 19:17; 1 John 3:13.

Healing: Psa. 103:3; Isa. 53:5; Matt. 8:16, 17; 10:1, 7, 8; 15:29-31; 17:14-21; Mark 16:14-20; Luke 9:1, 2, 6; Acts 19:11, 12; Jas. 5:14, 15; 1 Pet. 2:24.

Holy Spirit: Ezek. 36:26, 27; Joel 2:28, 29; Matt. 3:11, 16; Luke 11:11-13; 24:49; John 1:32, 33; 14:26; 15:26; 16:7-15; Acts 1:8; 2:4, 6, 7; 2:38, 39; 8:14-20; 9:17; 10:38; 11:15-17; 19:6; Rom. 5:5; 8:11, 16, 26; 12:5-8; 1 Cor. 2:10-14; 12:4-11; 2 Cor. 3:17; Gal. 3:2; 5:22, 23; 2 Pet. 1:21.

Humility: Prov. 15:33; 18:12; 22:4; Isa. 57:15; 66:2; Matt. 20:26-28; Luke 14:11; Jas. 4:6, 10.

Integrity: Job 2:3; 27:5; Psa. 7:8; 25:21; 26:1; Prov. 11:3.

Jealousy: Prov. 6:34; Song of Solomon 8:6.

Jesus: prophecies of, Isa. 7:14; 9:6; 53.

preexistence of, John 1:1-3; 8:58; 17:5; Col. 1:15-17.

divinity of, Matt. 1:18-25.

humanity of, Luke 22:44; 24:40-43; John 4:6; 11:35; Phil. 2:5-8; Heb. 4:15.

ministry of, Matt. 3:11; 5:17; 18:11; 20:28; Luke 4:18, 19; John 3:16, 17; Gal. 1:3, 4; 1 Tim. 1:15; Heb. 2:14, 15; 1 John 3:5-8.

second coming of, signs of, Dan. 7:13; Matt. 24:30 (read whole chapter); Luke 17:26-37; Acts 1:11; 1 Thess. 4:16, 17; 2 Thess. 2:1-4; 2 Tim. 3:1-5; 2 Pet. 3:3-10.

Kindness: Psa. 25:6; 36:7; 117:2; Isa. 54:8, 10; Jer. 9:24; 32:18.

Loneliness: Gen. 28:15; Psa. 68:6; John 14:18; Col. 2:10; Jas. 4:8.

Love: Deut. 10:12; Prov. 8:17; Matt. 10:37; 22:36-40; Luke 6:31-35; John 3:16; 13:34, 35; 14:21-24; 16:27; Rom. 5:8; 13:8-10; 1 Cor. 13; 16:22; Gal. 5:14; 2 Tim. 2:24, 25; 1 Pet. 3:8; 4:8; 1 John 3:11-23; 4:7-21.

Mercy: Num. 14:18; Psa. 23:6; 25:10; 57:3; 86:5; 103:17; Jer. 3:12; Mic. 6:8; Matt. 5:7; Luke 6:36; 2 Cor. 1:3; 4:1; Col. 3:12; Jas. 2:13; 5:11.

Mind, the: doubtful, Luke 12:29-31; Rom. 14:23; Jas. 1:8.

carnal, Rom. 8:6, 7.

blinded, 2 Cor. 3:14; 4:3, 4.

defiled, Mark 7:14-23; Titus 1:15.

renewed, Rom. 8:6; 12:2; Eph. 4:21-24; Phil. 2:5.

reprobate, Rom. 1:28-32.

Miracles: Mark 6:52; 9:39; John 2:11; 6:26; 11:47; Acts 2:22; 4:16; 6:8; 19:11; 1 Cor. 12:10, 28, 29; Gal. 3:5; Heb. 2:4.

Needs: material, Deut. 30:9, 10; Psa. 23:1; 37:4, 5, 25; 84:11; Isa. 41:17-20; Jer. 32:17, 27; Matt. 6:25-34; Phil. 4:19; Heb. 13:5, 6.

spiritual, Deut. 4:29; Psa. 37:4-6; Prov. 10:24; Isa. 44:3; 55:1-3; Jer. 29:11-13; Matt. 5:6; John 6:35; Heb. 4:16; Jas. 4:8.

Obedience: to God, Deut. 11:26-28; 1 Sam. 15:22; Isa. 48:18; Jer. 7:23; John 14:15, 21; Acts 5:29; 1 John 2:3-6; Rev. 22:14.

to others, Matt. 22:17-21; Rom. 13:1-7; Col. 3:22-24; Titus 3:1; 1 Pet. 2:13-20.

to parents, Eph. 6:1; Col. 3:20.

Occult, the: Lev. 19:31; 20:27; Deut. 18:10-12; 1 Chron. 10:13, 14; 2 Chron. 33:6; Isa. 8:19; Jer. 27:9; 1 Tim. 4:1; 2 Tim. 4:1-4; Rev. 21:8.

Overcomers: John 16:33; Rev. 2:7, 11, 17, 26; 3:5, 12, 21.

Patience: Psalm 37:7; 40:1; Rom. 5:3-5; 12:10-12; Phil. 4:11, 12; Heb. 6:12; 10:35, 36; Jas. 1:3, 4; 5:7, 8; 2 Pet. 1:5-7.

Peace: Psa. 119:165; Isa. 26:3; 32:17; 48:18; John 14:27; 16:33; Rom. 8:6; Phil. 4:6, 7.

Praise: Psa. 22:3; 34:1; 50:23; 100:4; Prov. 27:21; Isa. 42:8; 43:21; Luke 2:13, 20; Acts 2:47; Heb. 13:15; 1 Pet. 2:9.

Prayer: Job 42:10; Psa. 42:5; 50:15; 66:18; Prov. 28:9; Isa. 1:11-15; 40:31; 55:6, 7; 59:1, 2; Jer. 29:12, 13; 33:3; Lam. 3:25, 26; Dan. 10:12, 13; Matt. 6:5-8; 18:19; 21:21, 22; 26:41; Mark 9:23; 11:21-24; Luke 18:1; 21:36; John 9:31; 15:7; Phil. 4:6, 7; 1 Thess. 5:17; 1 Tim. 2:8; Heb. 11:6; Jas. 1:6-8; 1 John 3:21, 22; 5:14, 15.

Pride: Prov. 6:16-19; 11:2; 16:18; 29:23; Jer. 9:23, 24; Matt. 5:3, 5; 6:1-4; 20:26, 27; Luke 14:11; Jas. 4:6.

Prosperity: Josh. 1:7-9; 1 Sam. 2:7; Psa. 37:7; Rom. 9:17-24; 3 John 2.

Protection: Psa. 91; 121; Prov. 3:24-26; 29:25; Isa. 43:2; Jer. 15:20, 21.

Rewards: 2 Chron. 15:7; Psa. 58:11; Isa. 40:10; Jer. 17:10; Matt. 16:27; Mark 9:41; Luke 6:35; 1 Cor. 3:8, 13, 15; Gal. 6:7-9; Col. 3:24, 25; Heb. 10:36; 11:6; Rev. 20:12; 22:12.

Salvation: Matt. 3:1, 2; Luke 15:10; John 3:16; 5:24; 10:27, 28; Acts 2:38, 39; 3:19; Rom. 2:4; 6:23; 10:9, 10; Eph. 2:8, 9; 2 Tim. 1:9; 1 Pet. 1:3-5; 2 Pet. 3:9; 1 John 1:9; 2:25; 5:13.

Satan: Job 1:6-12; 2:3-7; Isa. 14:12-17; Ezek. 28:13-19; Matt. 17:14-18; Luke 4:1-3; 10:18; 13:16; John 8:44; Acts 5:3; 2 Cor. 4:4; 11:3; Eph. 4:27; 6:11-18; Col. 1:13; 2:15; 1 Thess. 2:18; Heb. 2:14; Jas. 4:7; 1 Pet. 5:8, 9; 1 John 3:8; 4:4; Rev. 12:9, 10; 20:10.

Sin: Mal. 3:5; Matt. 9:13; Rom. 1:21-32; 5:8; 1 Cor. 6:9, 10, 15-18; Gal. 5:16-21; Eph. 5:5; Jas. 4:4; 1 John 1:8, 10; Rev. 21:8.

Sorrow: Psa. 30:5; 119:50; 126:5, 6; Isa. 40:1, 2; 66:13; Jer. 31:13; Matt. 5:4; Rev. 21:4.

Strife: Prov. 15:18; 16:28; 20:3; 28:25; 29:22; 30:33; Phil. 2:3; 1 Tim. 6:4; Jas. 3:14.

Suffering: Rom. 8:16-18; 1 Cor. 12:25, 26; 2 Tim. 2:12; 3:12; Heb. 2:10; 1 Pet. 1:11; 2:19; 5:1.

Temperance: Acts 24:25; 1 Cor. 9:25; Gal. 5:23; Titus 1:8; 2:2; 2 Pet. 1:6.

Temptation: Mark 14:38; 1 Cor. 10:13; 1 Tim. 6:9, 10; Jas. 1:2-4, 12, 13-15; 1 Pet. 1:6, 7; 2 Pet. 2:9.

Thoughts: Prov. 23:7; 24:9; Isa. 55:8; 66:18; Matt. 15:19; 2 Cor. 10:5; Phil. 4:8; Jas. 2:4.

Unselfishness: Prov. 19:17; 21:13; Rom. 15:1; Gal. 6:2; Phil. 2:3, 4; 1 Thess. 5:14; Heb. 13:2, 3.

Vengeance: Deut. 32:35, 43; Prov. 20:22; Luke 18:7, 8; Rom. 12:17-19; Heb. 10:30.

Wisdom: Psa. 111:10; Prov. 2:6-11; 3:13-18; 4:5-9; Luke 21:15; Jas. 1:5-7.

Worry: Prov. 16:3; Matt. 6:25, 34; Mark 13:11; Luke 12:22.

Recommended Reading

Abrahamson, E. M., and Pezet, A. W. *Body, Mind, and Sugar.* New York: Avon Books, 1977.

Abramson, Edward. *Behavioral Approaches to Weight Control.* New York: Springer, 1977.

Adams, Ruth, and Murray, Frank. *Is Blood Sugar Making You a Nutritional Cripple?* New York: Larchmont Books, 1975.

Airola, Paavo. *How to Get Well.* Phoenix: Health Plus, 1974.

————. *Hypoglycemia: A Better Approach.* Phoenix: Health Plus, 1977.

Bakker, Jim and Tammy. *How We Lost Weight and Kept It Off!* Harrison, Ark.: New Leaf Press, 1979.

Basansky, Bill. *The Land of Milk and Honey.* Tulsa: Bill Basansky Ministries, 1977.

Bauer, J. *Clinical Laboratory Methods.* St. Louis: C. V. Mosby Company, 1982.

Beck, Aaron. *Cognitive Therapy and the Emotional Disorders.* New York: New American Library, 1979.

Benson, Herbert, and Klipper, Miriam. *The Relaxation Response.* Glasgow: Fountain Books, 1977.

Benson, Herbert. *The Mind/Body Effect.* New York: Berkley Books, 1980.

Bragg, Paul C. and Patricia. *The Shocking Truth About Water.* Santa Barbara: Health Science, 1977.

Brandt, Frans M. J. *A Rational Self-Counseling Primer.* Charlottesville, Va.: Rational Self-Counseling Institutes, 1979.

———. *A Guide to Rational Weight Control.* Oscoda, Mich.: Wesselhoeft Associates, 1980.

———. "How to Heal Depression." *Journal of the National Council of Psychotherapists.* Vol. X, No. 2. London, 1983.

———. "Rational Self-Counseling: Thinking About Our Thinking." *Journal of the National Council of Psychotherapists,* Vol. VII, No. 4. London, 1980.

Bredesen, Harold, and Scheer, James. *Need a Miracle?* Old Tappan, N.J.: Fleming H. Revell, 1979.

Brennan, R. O. *Nutrigenetics.* New York: New American Library, 1975.

Bricklin, Mark. *Natural Healing Cookbook.* Emmaus, Penn.: Rodale Press, 1981.

Brown, B. *Your Words Are Your Magic Power.* New York: Simon & Schuster, 1971.

Buchman, Dian. *Herbal Medicine.* New York: Gramercy Publishing Company, 1980.

Burns, David. *Feeling Good: The New Mood Therapy.* New York: William Morrow, 1980.

Capps, Charles. *The Tongue: A Creative Force.* Tulsa: Harrison House, 1977.

Carlson, Ronald. *Transcendental Meditation: Relaxation or Religion?* Chicago: Moody Press, 1978.

Cheraskin, Emanuel. *New Hope for Incurable Diseases.* New York: Arco, 1971.

Cleave, T. *The Saccharine Disease.* New Canaan, Conn.: Keats, 1975.

Coca, Arthur. *The Pulse Test.* New York: Arco, 1979.

Conn, H. *Four Trojan Horses.* Van Nuys, Calif.: Bible Voice, 1978.

Davis, Adelle. *Let's Get Well.* New York: Signet, 1972.

Davis, Francyne. *The Low Blood Sugar Cookbook.* New York: Bantam, 1974.

Dearing, Trevor. *Supernatural Healing Today.* Plainfield, N.J.: Logos International, 1979.

Diamond, John. *Your Body Doesn't Lie.* New York: Warner Books, 1980.

Dufty, William. *Sugar Blues.* New York: Warner Books, 1976.

Eareckson, Joni. *Joni.* Grand Rapids, Mich.: Zondervan, 1976.

Eby, F. *Champions Forever.* Coldwater, Mich.: Eagle Printing, 1978.

Fredericks, Carlton. *Low Blood Sugar and You.* New York: Charter Books, 1969.

Freedman, J. *Happy People.* New York: Ballantine, 1980.

Frost, Robert C. *Aglow with the Spirit.* Plainfield, N.J.: Logos International, 1965.

———. *The Biology of the Holy Spirit.* Old Tappan, N.J.: Fleming H. Revell, 1975.

Gilquist, Peter. *Let's Quit Fighting About the Holy Spirit.* Grand Rapids, Mich.: Zondervan, 1974.

Glasser, William. *Reality Therapy.* New York: Perennial Library, 1975.

Graedon, Joe. *The People's Pharmacy.* New York: Avon Books, 1977.

———. *The People's Pharmacy 2.* New York: Avon Books, 1980.

Graham, Billy. *The Holy Spirit.* Waco, Tex.: Word Books, 1978.

———. *Till Armageddon.* Waco, Tex.: Word Books, 1981.

Hagin, Kenneth. *Exceedingly Growing Faith.* Tulsa: Kenneth Hagin Ministries, 1978.

———. *Words.* Tulsa: Kenneth Hagin Ministries, 1979.

Hauck, P. *Overcoming Depression.* Philadelphia: The Westminster Press, 1976.

Horton, Harold. *The Gifts of the Spirit.* Springfield, Mo.: Gospel Publishing House, 1975.

Hunter, Frances. *God's Answer to Fat . . . Loose It.* Houston: Hunter Ministries Publishing Company, 1975.

Hurdle, J. Frank. *A Country Doctor's Common Sense Health Manual.* West Nyack, N.Y.: Parker Publishing Company, 1975.

Johnson, Wendell. *People in Quandaries.* New York: Harper & Row, 1946.

Kaufman, William. *The Sugar-Free Cookbook.* Garden City, N.Y.: Doubleday, 1964.

Kirban, Salem. *The Getting Back to Nature Diet.* Irvine, Calif.: Harvest House, 1978.

Krieger, Dolores. *The Therapeutic Touch.* Englewood Cliffs, N.J.: Prentice-Hall, 1979.

LaHaye, Tim. *How to Win over Depression.* Grand Rapids, Mich.: Zondervan, 1974.

Lewis, C. S. *Mere Christianity.* New York: Macmillan, 1943.

Light, M. *Homeostasis Revisited.* Troy, N.Y.: Hypoglycemia Foundation, Inc., 1981.

———. *Hypoglycemia.* Troy, N.Y.: Hypoglycemia Foundation, Inc., 1982.

Linn, Dennis, and Linn, Matthew. *Healing of Memories.* New York: Paulist Press, 1974.

Lovett. C. S. *Jesus Wants You Well.* Baldwin Park, Calif.: Personal Christianity, 1973.

Mackarness, R. *Eat Fat and Grow Slim.* Glasgow: William Collins & Company, 1975.

———. *Not All in the Mind.* London: Pan Books, 1976.

———. *Chemical Victims.* London: Pan Books, 1980.

MacMillen, S. I. *None of These Diseases.* Old Tappan, N.J.: Spire Books, 1963.

MacNutt, Francis. *Healing.* New York: Bantam Books, 1977.

———. *The Power to Heal.* New York: Bantam Books, 1979.

Mallough, Don. *Living by Faith.* Springfield, Mo.: Gospel Publishing House, 1978.

Mandell, Marshall, and Scanlon, Lynne. *Dr. Mandell's Five-Day Allergy Relief System.* New York: Pocket Books, 1980.

Marshall, Catherine. *The Helper.* New York: Avon Books, 1978.

Maultsby, Maxie. *Help Yourself to Happiness Through Rational Self-Counseling.* Boston: Marlborough House, 1975.

———. *A Million Dollars for Your Hangover.* Lexington, Ken.: Rational Self-Help Books, 1978.

———. *Rational Behavior Therapy.* Englewood Cliffs, N.J.: Prentice-Hall, 1984.

Narramore, Clyde and Ruth. *How to Handle Pressure.* Wheaton, Ill.: Tyndale House, 1975.

Nelson, C. Ellis. *Don't Let Your Conscious Be Your Guide.* New York: Paulist Press, 1978.

Page, Melvin. *Your Body Is Your Best Doctor.* New Canaan, Conn.: Keats Publishing, 1972.

Peale, Norman Vincent. *The Power of Positive Thinking.* New York: Fawcett Crest, 1980.

———. *The Positive Power of Jesus Christ.* Wheaton, Ill.: Tyndale House, 1980.

———. *The Positive Principle Today.* Englewood Cliffs, N.J.: Prentice-Hall, 1976.

———, and Blanton, Smiley. *Faith Is the Answer.* New York: Fawcett Crest, 1979.

Powell, John. *He Touched Me.* Allen, Tex.: Argus Communications, 1974.

———. *Fully Human, Fully Alive.* Allen, Tex.: Argus Communications, 1976.

Prince, Derek. *Prayer and Fasting.* Old Tappan, N.J.: Fleming H. Revell, 1973.

———. *Faith to Live by.* Ann Arbor, Mich.: Servant Books, 1977.

Rosenfeld, Isadore. *Second Opinion.* New York: Simon & Schuster, 1981.

Sanford, Agnes. *The Healing Light.* Plainfield, N.J.: Logos International, 1972.

Saunders, Jeraldine, and Ross, Harvey. *Hypoglycemia: The Disease Your Doctor Won't Treat.* Los Angeles: Pinnacle Books, 1980.

Schaeffer, Francis. *The Mark of a Christian.* Downers Grove, Ill.: InterVarsity Press, 1970.

Schuller, Robert. *Self-Love.* New York: Hawthorn Books, 1969.

———. *Reach out for New Life.* New York: Bantam Books, 1977.

———. *Discover Your Possibilities.* New York: Ballantine, 1979.

Selye, Hans. *The Stress of Life.* New York: McGraw-Hill, 1978.

Sheinkin, David, and Schacter, M. *Food, Mind & Mood.* New York: Warner Books, 1980.

Smith, Lendon. *Feed Your Kids Right.* New York: Delta Books, 1979.

Somekh, Emile. *The Complete Guide to Children's Allergies.* Los Angeles: Pinnacle Books, 1980.

Stapleton, Ruth Carter. *The Gift of Inner Healing.* Waco, Tex.: Word, 1976.

————. *In His Footsteps.* San Francisco: Harper & Row, 1979.

Stearns, Frederic. *Anger.* Springfield, Ill.: Charles C. Thomas, 1972.

Stutman, Fred. *The Doctor's Walking Book.* New York: Ballantine, 1980.

Ten Boom, Corrie. *The Hiding Place.* New York: Bantam Books, 1974.

————. *Prison Letters.* Old Tappan, N.J.: Fleming H. Revell, 1975.

Tintera, J. "Endocrine Aspects of Schizophrenia: Hypoglycemia or Hypoadrenocorticism." *Journal of Schizophrenia.* Vol. 1, No. 3, 1967.

Tintera, J., and H. Lovell. "Endocrine Treatment of Alcoholism." *Geriatrics.* Vol. 4, No. 5, 1949.

Tintera, J. "The Hypoadrenocortical State and Its Management." *New York State Journal of Medicine.* Vol. 55, No. 13, 1955.

Tintera, J., and H. Lovell, "Hypoadrenocorticism in Alcoholism and Drug addiction." *Geriatrics.* Vol. 6, No. 1, 1951.

Trintera, J. "Stabilizing Homeostasis in the Recovered Alcoholic Through Endocrine Therapy: Evalucation of the Hypoglycemia Factor." *Journal of American Geriatrics Society.* Vol. 14, No. 2, 1966.

Trine, Ralph. *In Tune with the Infinite.* London: G. Bell and Sons, 1977.

Vaux, K. *This Mortal Coil.* San Francisco: Harper & Row, 1978.

Vitz, Paul. *Psychology as Religion: The Cult of Self-Worship.* Grand Rapids, Mich.: Wm. B. Eerdmans, 1977.

Whittlesey, Marietta. *Killer Salt.* New York: Avon Books, 1978.

Wilkerson, David. *Suicide.* Old Tappan, N.J.: Fleming H. Revell, 1978.

Williams, Roger J. *Alcoholism: The Nutritional Approach.* Austin, Tex.: University of Texas Press, 1976.

Winter, Ruth. *A Consumer's Dictionary of Food Additives.* New York: Crown Publishers, 1978.

Wright, Jonathan V. *Dr. Wright's Book of Nutritional Therapy.* Emmaus, Penn.: Rodale Press, 1979.